THE FASCIST TRADITION

MAJOR TRADITIONS OF WORLD CIVILIZATION

UNDER THE EDITORSHIP OF HAYDEN V. WHITE

THE FASCIST TRADITION

RADICAL RIGHT-WING EXTREMISM IN MODERN EUROPE

JOHN WEISS
Associate Professor of Modern European History
Wayne State University

HARPER & ROW, PUBLISHERS
NEW YORK, EVANSTON, AND LONDON

 For information address Harper & Row, Publishers, Incorporated, 49 East 33rd Street, New York, N.Y. 10016.

Library of Congress Catalog Card Number: 67-17642

CONTENTS

EDITOR'S INTRODUCTION

What is the "true" nature of fascism: is it something radically new to political experience, a unique creation of the twentieth century; or is it merely old tyranny possessed of new, more efficient techniques for gaining and holding power? Historians, sociologists, social psychologists, and political theorists have been debating this question since Mussolini's seizure of power in 1922. Thus far, however, with limited success. On the whole, we have not arrived at any general consensus over the nature and causes of fascism in our time.

The reasons for our disagreements are easy to discern. They lie in the ideological differences which separate the radical from the conservative in the political arena and in the bad conscience which many present-day liberals feel for their failure to anticipate the advent of fascism and to oppose it effectively once it had made its appearance in the 1920s and 1930s.

For the conventional liberal, with his late nineteenth century notions of human nature, society, and the historical process, the triumph of fascism in Italy and Germany seemed to refute many of his most cherished preconceptions. It certainly dashed many of his fondest hopes for the future of Western civilization. After all, fascism had succeeded, not in the backward and underdeveloped areas of the world, but in two of the most advanced nations of Western Europe. Italy and Germany had made lasting contributions to Western civilization in its modern form: Italy by the Renaissance, Germany by the Reformation. Their national cultural traditions stood for two of the West's most highly prized ideals: that of freedom of religious conscience and that of the dignity of man. Moreover, although their development into "modern" nations had been slow, by the end of the nineteenth century, both Italy and Germany had given every evidence of being able to transform themselves into "enlightened" social systems. By the beginning of the twentieth century, in fact, both countries seemed to have yielded to liberal arguments and criticism, and each seemed at last to have entered into the European community of nations as a full-fledged and responsible member. Why, then, liberals had to ask themselves, had Italy and Germany suddenly and unexpectedly retrogressed into a barbarism made all the more barbarous by the instruments of violence and thought control which their technical, economic, and scientific advancement had accorded them? Was there something inherently wrong with them as nations? Did the trouble lie in the very concept of progress itself? Or was there something inherently vicious about the process of liberalization in the modern context?

When liberals began to ask these questions, two answers were already available for consideration. On the one side, Marxist critics held that fascism was an inevitable outcome of the capitalist system, a necessary response of a decadent middle class to the loss of colonial markets abroad and to the pressure of a growing, revolutionary proletariat at home. Lenin had laid the groundwork for this view in his writings on imperialism, and the Marxists of the 'twenties and 'thirties had merely to extend his thesis to encompass fascism as an expression of the death-gasp of capitalism. This interpretation had the merit of simplicity, and it convinced many radicals who were not Marxist in their basic postures. It remained the most popular explanation of the appearance of fascism in Italy and Germany down to the end of the second World War.

On the other side of the political spectrum, however, what seemed to be another interpretation soon appeared. This came from conservative humanist thinkers who regarded industrialism, science, rationalism, and democracy itself as the main threats to civilization as they conceived it. Invoking an idealized vision of pre-industrial society, these thinkers spoke of a time when men lived in close communion with nature, when social relationships had been simple, immediate, and governed by time-honored custom, and when public life had been informed by idealistic conceptions of honor, responsibility, and a fundamental respect for human dignity. By the lights of these thinkers, industrialism had brought rapid (too rapid) population expansion, urbanization, the massification of mankind, and the development of new techniques of mass persuasion and social disciplining. This had led, in turn, to a "revolt of the masses" and to the degradation of all those cultural values which had kept Western civilization on the course of progress and enlightenment at an appropriate pace since the Renaissance. Fascism, therefore, was merely the sign of the triumph of the new barbarians of the mass city over the cultivated, humanistically educated elites which had governed them since the beginnings of civilization. In short, and curiously, the Marxist and the conservative humanist interpretations of fascism converged: fascism, both agreed, was the necessary outcome of the rationalism, materialism, and insensitivity of bourgeois society. The principal difference between the Marxist interpretation of fascism and the conservative humanist view lay in what each regarded as the implications of fascism's triumph for the future—and the emotions which contemplation of the future inspired. Whereas Marxists saw in fascism a confirmation of Marxist philosophy of history, the conservative humanist saw in it a negation of history itself. And where the former saw the advent of fascism as merely a prelude to a freer, more noble age, a communistic age, the latter saw it as heralding the death of civilization itself.

More recently, scholars have been trying to find grounds for a position somewhere between these two extremes. Professor John Weiss, of Wayne State University's Department of History, belongs to this group of revisionists. To the question: What is the cause of fascism's triumph in Germany and Italy? his answer is that there is no single, simple explanation; but that, if we are to find an explanation, we shall do so only by analyzing *how fascism functions* in various societies, not by concentrating on what fascism's defenders and detractors *say* about it. In fine, Weiss holds that we shall comprehend fascism only by going beyond considerations of its putative ideological content to a study of the specific sociological, political, and economic conditions that breed it. And on the basis of such a study, he concludes that fascism, far from being the last phase of liberalism, is the peculiarly twentieth century response of conservative groups threatened by rapid liberalization of the social system in which they enjoy a privileged place. Thus, fascism is, in his view, primarily another manifestation of the Radical Right in the political spectrum, a new expression of a tradition of thought and action with a long history in Western (and also in Eastern) culture. It is this conception of fascism as the modern form of right-wing extremist politics which allows him to speak of a "fascist tradition."

By taking this line of argument, Weiss is permitted

to by-pass all of those interpretations of German Nazism and Italian Fascism which, on grounds similar to those invoked by fascists themselves, view totalitarianism as an inherent national trait. For some time now, the lay public has been told that Nazism was a uniquely German phenomenon, a peculiar expression of a barbarism intrinsic to the German national character, and an inevitable consequence of Germany's attainment of political autonomy. This conception of the growth of fascism in Germany overlooks the fact that fascism has made its appearance in other countries and that the conditions which bred fascism in Germany and Italy were (and still are) potentially present in France, England, and even the United States. Weiss holds that, if we are to understand fascism as a *historical phenomenon,* that is, as a movement which did crystallize in Italy and Germany in the twentieth century, but for which there were no compelling reasons for predicting its triumph there prior to the events themselves, then we must follow the course of its emergence out of situations which have been developing in Western Europe since the French Revolution.

After granting the *partial* validity of earlier interpretations of fascism, Weiss turns to a consideration of fascism's ideological content. And he characterizes the ideas and ideals upon which fascists conventionally draw as the following:

1) organicist conceptions of community;

2) philosophical idealism;

3) idealization of "manly" (usually peasant or village) virtues;

4) hostility to advanced, corporation or monopoly capitalism;

5) a resentment of mass democracy;

6) elitist conceptions of political and social leadership;

7) racism, and usually, though not necessarily, anti-semitism;

8) militarism; and

9) imperialism.

All of these components, he suggests, have one thing in common: hostility to liberal values and institutions. They crystallize in a distinctly fascist movement, he maintains, when they are combined with an effort to gain *mass support* and when they are combined with a decision to use *extreme violence* and sophisticated methods of *thought control* to gain such support. He grants that once fascists are in power they often appear to be "qualitatively" different from their nineteenth century forebears, but he finds this qualitative difference to reside solely in the extremist means fascists employ to achieve their goals, not in the nature of the goals themselves. This extremism, in turn, seems justified to traditional conservatives who feel threatened by the liberalism and socialism that usually accompany industrialization and modernization of any social system. Thus, Weiss denies that fascism can be explained as a "revolt of irrationalists" against science and technology; from the standpoint of conservatives under siege from the Left, fascism appears as a perfectly "rational" solution to the problems besetting them. In sum, within the context of a rapidly industrializing, urbanizing, and democratizing social system, entrenched conservatives *may* opt for fascist methods—violence, thought control, terror, and even genocide—in the hope of saving whatever they can of their received way of life, privileges, and class values.

That such an option is not inevitable Weiss shows by his analysis of the career of fascism in different countries. In his discussion of fascist takeovers in Germany and Italy, he shows that these were not true "seizures of power," but rather consequences of political coalitions between various elements *within* the political Right and between the Right and those groups that stood to lose most by the triumph of liberalism or socialism, that is, small artisans, small business men, deracinated aristocrats, etc. His point is that fascism is a threat mainly in those societies that have made a start in transforming themselves into *modern* social systems. Precisely because Germany and Italy had entered upon processes of industrialization and liberalization, they were exposed to that polarization of classes which is the *sine qua non* of fascist growth. Because there were strong liberal and socialist movements in Germany and Italy, conservatives in those countries correctly saw in the growth of the Left a threat to their own survival. This gave to them the incentive to try fascist "total solutions" to their problems when all else failed.

However, once fascists came to power in Germany and Italy, they overrode their conservative sponsors and faulted on the "social welfare" promises they had made on their supporters in the masses. This was an eventuality which neither the conservative elites nor the bewildered mass electorates could have foreseen. Hitler above all grasped the potentialities for gaining complete control of the social system offered by modern methods of communication and transportation and police agencies. And this "run away" aspect of fascism is analyzed in Weiss's account of the Radical Right in power. Here he argues that Nazism at least was no mere conservative ideology in practice but a sustained assault on civilization in all its forms, liberal, conservative, and radical.

That fascism of the Hitler variety is not an inevitable option of conservative classes under siege from the Left is shown by Weiss's analysis of fascism in England, Spain, and Hungary. He suggests that the fate of fascist movements in these countries provide negative confirmations of his thesis, for in these countries the strength of of fascists and the extent of their extremist programs varied in direct proportion to the threat from the liberal or socialist opposition. Where liberal institutions and values were most firmly established, as in Britain, fascism remained little more than an aberration. In Spain, where conservative groups were stronger but where genuine liberal and socialist groups existed in opposition, the conservative response was stronger. But once liberals and socialists had been defeated, fascist techniques were used primarily for supporting the older, conservative order, not in the radically uprooting way that they were used in Germany. Finally, in Hungary, where socialist forces were weak and only temporarily successful, the response of conservatives was correspondingly moderate in what they permitted of their fascist pawns. We may conclude from all this that fascism, though a product of global forces in an age of transition from agrarian to industrial social systems, was neither a *necessary* outcome of any given national experience nor an *inevitable* stage in the evolution of liberal democracies, although it remains a distinct *possibility* for any society undergoing such processes. This conclusion sets the stage for Weiss's concluding speculations.

Quite simply, Weiss holds that the future of fascism, if it has one, is in the underdeveloped but emerging nations of the world. In order to exist in the modern world, nations like Rhodesia, South Africa, and many of the Latin American countries must industrialize. By industrialization, however, they create the conditions within which a liberal or socialist movement can take shape. These movements, in turn, inevitably threaten established groups and classes, thereby throwing them open to the anxieties that breed contemplation of a fascist program that will allow them to enjoy the privileges of the old order and the advantages of the new simultaneously. In short, in the non-Western world, the immediate danger is not a totalitarianism of the Left but of the Right. And Weiss's implication is that Westerners who understand correctly how fascism is born out of the conflict between established conservative groups and the justified aspirations of new groups created by industrialization, will be able sagely to dispense their aid and comfort to those who seek a middle way between the totalitarianisms of both the Left and the Right. His study of fascism, therefore, leaves us precisely where any serious historical work ought to leave us: in the present, with our problems illuminated and our tasks clarified.

HAYDEN V. WHITE

CHRONOLOGY OF EVENTS RELATIVE TO FASCISM IN MODERN TIMES

ITALY

1870	The unification of the Kingdom of Italy under Cavour and King Victor Emmanuel.
1892–1893	The first ministry of Giovanni Giolitti, whose conservative-liberal character was to be the major personal political force in Italy until World War I.
1896 March 1	The battle of Adua. Italian troops suffered a disastrous defeat and Italy was forced to recognize Ethiopian independence. The responsible minister, Crispi, fell, and Italy's hope for an African Empire was shattered. Crispi became somewhat of a hero to the Italian right and, later, fascism.
1898	Bread riots led to martial law and the brief rule of General Luigi Pelloux who took extreme measures against liberals and radicals. A liberal-left coalition succeeded in defending the Constitution and causing the fall of this first modern embodiment of military and authoritarian conservatism in Italy.
1900 July 29	King Humbert was assassinated by an anarchist, and succeeded by King Victor Emmanuel III.
1901	Strikes and the growth of socialism gave evidence of the new vigor of liberalism and leftism.
1904	General strike proclaimed: The church joined in earnest the right's struggle against liberalism and radicalism. Pope Pius X lifted the boycott against Catholics partaking in Italian politics.

	Catholic political activity was encouraged by the church if it aided the Italian right.
1908	Reformists and revisionists in the Socialist party succeeded in expelling revolutionary syndicalists from the party.
1909	Benito Mussolini, age 25, a Socialist of the revolutionary left, became the editor of a small revolutionary paper, *Lotta di Classe*.
1911	Tripolitan War with Turkey: the war was strongly supported by the intellectuals of the newly formed and radical right Nationalist party (1910) of Enrico Corradini and Gabriele D'Annunzio. This party had a strong following in both the army and heavy industry. The Italians gained a dubious empire in Tripoli and the Dodecanese Islands. (Though relatively unnoticed at the time, perhaps one of the most important historical markers of modern time was passed when an Italian officer and pilot bombed a group of helpless Arabs from the then newly invented airplane.)
1911	Mussolini was jailed for five months for agitating against the war.
1912	In a startling reversal of fortune, the reformists were expelled from the Italian Socialist party by its revolutionary left wing. Mussolini, one of the leaders of the revolutionists, was given the editorship of the important and official party paper, *Avanti*.
1912 June 29	The franchise was extended from three to eight million voters. Universal suffrage was close to completion. This, plus the revolutionary direction of the growing Socialist movement, provoked a rightist reaction among the establishment.
1913	The conservative rulers of Italy saw the handwriting on the wall with the elections of 1913. Radical liberals won 70 seats, liberals gained a majority, and the Socialists almost doubled their

	seats. One-quarter of the nation voted for socialism.
1913	Mussolini, running as a Socialist native-son candidate in Forli, lost badly, perhaps because of his connections with the revolutionary left.
1914 March	Salandra, an authoritarian reactionary, succeeded Giolitti as first Minister.
1914 June 7	"Red Week"—police and antimilitarist demonstrators clashed, and police brutality led to trade union, Socialist, and syndicalist support for a general strike. The red flag was raised in many communities, republics were proclaimed, generals were jailed, churches were burned, and looting occurred. Mussolini, still supporting peasants and workers, played a prominent role in the disturbances. The right won, however, and Salandra remained in power.
1914 August 3	With the outbreak of World War I, Salandra declared Italy's neutrality.
1914	Mussolini took a prowar stand and was expelled from the Socialist party and the editorship of *Avanti.*
1915	Mussolini tentatively began his long journey to the right by gaining his own paper, a paper subsidized by France and those who wished to bring Italy into the war—circles close to king, court, army, nationalists, and imperialists.
1915 May	Italy mobilized and declared war on Austria-Hungary. (Italy did not declare war on Germany until August 28th, 1916). Italy entered partly because of agreements with the Western Allies that territory should be transferred from Austria-Hungary to Italy upon victory. Conservative nationalists saw visions of an Italian Slavic-African Empire at Austrian and Turkish expense.
1917 February	Mussolini was wounded as a result of an accident at the Front, and he returned to his journalistic activities. He recommenced as well his rightward

	movement toward nationalism, imperialism, and the glorification of the military virtues.
1918	Armistice, November, 1918: At the Treaty and peace conferences, President Wilson set himself against Orlando's claims as to the distribution of territory between Italy and Yugoslavia. Italy lost some of what it claimed. Because Orlando was a liberal, Italy's loss was used (as was Germany's in Weimar later) as evidence for the bankruptcy and treason of liberals, with regard to the "sacred cause of the nation." D'Annunzio led—and Mussolini followed—in the cry of "Fiume or Death."
1919	Inflation, unemployment, worker and peasant unrest, and an apparently pointless and massive sacrifice of life in the war led to postwar crises.
1919 March 23	The Fascist party was founded by Mussolini in Milan. The first programs of the party showed that Mussolini still hoped to gain a political victory through the uniting of opposites from both left and right. His program contained elements appealing to unemployed workers, war veterans, landowners, industrialists, imperialists, and landless peasants. "We are reactionaries and revolutionaries, aristocrats and democrats, conservatives and progressives."
1919	D'Annunzio and his proto-Fascists seized Fiume by force to the chagrin of the Italian government (Nitti). Fiume held illegally for about a year. D'Annunzio was one of those left or idealistic fascists who *did* want to implement some measure of social justice for workers and peasants. For this reason (and others) he lost the kind of support of conservative wealth and influence which Mussolini and Hitler were to gain.
1919 November	Perhaps the most crucial elections ever held in Italy: The Socialists became the largest parliamentary party. The middle groups began to disintegrate. The rulers of Italy now knew that radical social and economic reform would be their fate should parliamentary democracy con-

	tinue. The Fascists were completely defeated, as was Mussolini himself. From this, Mussolini learned that to gain power, left fascism must be discarded.
1920 Summer and Fall	Workers' strikes, occupation of factories, and peasant-land seizures mounted to a crescendo. Mussolini cemented his allegiance to the right as his street toughs answered the left with terror.
1921	Giolitti made election agreements with Mussolini in the hope of weakening the left and, following a conservative precedent, planned to use the radical right without being controlled by them. The Fascists won 35 seats; their allies, 10—the Socialists were still the largest parliamentary party.
1921 November	The National Congress of the Fascist party: Mussolini made it quite clear: Fascism is revolutionary conservatism. He spoke of his support for the army, landowners, monarchy, industry, nationalism, and the sanctity of private property.
1922	The Blackshirts, aided by the army and the police, seized municipalities and cities.
1922 October 27	The march on Rome: Facta (Prime Minister) and Victor Emmanuel III agreed to cooperate; and, again with the support of the army and police, Mussolini and his Blackshirts were given power to stop the left.
1922–1924	Mussolini consolidated his rule according to normal despotic practice. Bureaucracy and police were purged, Mussolini was granted exceptional powers, a Fascist Grand Council was set up, paramilitary units under Fascist control were formed, and election laws were passed to give fascism more parliamentary control.
1924 June	Matteotti, an exceptionally brave Socialist Deputy, exposed the electoral practices by which the Fascists had gained some 65 percent of the vote. He was murdered by Fascist toughs. The response of the still relatively free press, public,

	and parliament was such as to shock Mussolini into the realization that he could not expect to rule without total controls.
1924–1926	The creation of totalitarian institutions: The one-party state moved to total control over press, judiciary, educational, trade union, cultural, propaganda, and youth activities.
1926 April	The proclamation of the Corporate State: Officially, economic liberalism was cast aside in favor of government partnership with workers and owners for the social control of industry. Actually, as Mussolini himself later admitted, party agents worked at the behest of industrialist leaders, and the workers had no voice at all.
1929	The Lateran Accords: Mussolini and the Pope signed a Concordat in which the church finally made its peace with modern Italy. The papacy was given full territorial sovereignty over Vatican City, and Catholicism was affirmed as the "only state religion." The church later supported both Mussolini's Ethiopian war and his aid to Franco in Spain. The death of Pope Pius XI in 1939 may have prevented a break with the church, but Cardinal Pacelli, Pius XII, was obsessed with the need to destroy the Spanish Republic and hence allowed Mussolini to curb many anti-Fascist voices in his church.
1935 October	At the height of the Depression, Mussolini opened hostilities against Ethiopia. The League of Nations voted an embargo which, however, had small effect since no great power was willing to make concrete sacrifices to stop Italian imperialism in Africa.
1936	The Rome-Berlin Axis: Mussolini moved into Hitler's camp and agreed to the German remilitarization of the Rhineland. Thus Italy forsook its previous alliance with France and Great Britain.
1936	Mussolini sent 40,000 Italian troops and much

	material aid to General Franco and his right revolutionaries in Spain.
1938	Mussolini reluctantly agreed to Hitler's invasion of Austria. Italy deserted its previous role as the defender of Austria against German ambitions.
1938 September	Mussolini supported Hitler's move to take the Sudetenland from Czechoslovakia, and played the role of "honest broker" at the Munich Conference which saw Great Britain and France agree to Hitler's aggression.
1939 March	Hitler marched into Prague; Slovakia became a German protectorate; and Mussolini, if reluctantly, continued to support Hitler.
1939 April	Italian troops occupied Albania.
1939 May	German and Italian "Pact of Steel."
1939 September 1	Hitler invaded Poland. Great Britain and France declared war on Germany within hours of each other. Mussolini stayed out until June 10, 1940, when he joined the attack on an already defeated France.
1942 November	Allied landings in North Africa: The masses deserted Mussolini completely.
1943	Great workers' strikes against Mussolini: A resistance mounted by the left which was to reach large proportions.
1943 July 10	Italy invaded.
1943 July 24–25	The Fascist Grand Council and the King brought about the fall of Mussolini. Badoglio replaced him.
1943 September 12	Armistice between Italy and the Anglo-American forces, but the Germans continued the fight for Italy.
1943	Mussolini formed the Italian Social Republic at

	Salo on Lake Garda. A mere puppet of the Germans, Mussolini presented a pitiful figure as he returned to the "left fascism" of his youth and appealed to labor against the "plutocracy."
1945 April	Mussolini was captured and executed by partisans.

GERMANY

1871–1890	The rule of Bismarck and the Prussianization of Germany in the newly united and expanding German Empire.
1875	The Socialist Congress at Gotha united Marxists with the followers of Ferdinand Lassalle into the modern German Social Democratic Workingmen's party.
1876 October 18	At Bismarck's behest, severe anti-Socialist laws were passed which lasted until Bismarck's resignation in 1890. Meetings, publications, and the collection of money were forbidden if they were intended to further "social-democratic, socialist, or communistic designs" for the "overthrow of the state or society."
1883, 1884, 1889	With Bismarck leading, social welfare laws were passed which provided for sickness insurance, accident insurance, and age and invalidity insurance with joint contributions by workers, employers, and the state.
1888	Frederick III succeeded Wilhelm I, but Frederick, stricken with throat cancer, died within the year. He was succeeded by Wilhelm II.
1890 March 18	Bismarck resigned when he came into conflict with the young Emperor's relatively liberal views and desire for power.
1890–1913	Wilhelm II combined gradual liberalization at home with increasing imperialism and belligerency abroad.
1912 January	Elections to the *Reichstag* gave Socialists, now a reformist rather than revolutionary party, the

largest parliamentary representation and 4.5 million votes.

1914 June 28 through August 6	The outbreak of World War I, beginning with the assassination of Archduke Franz Ferdinand. Austria declared war on Serbia, July 28th. Germany declared war on Russia, August 1. Germany invaded Luxemburg, declared war on France (August 3rd), and invaded Belgium. England declared war on Germany, August 4th.
1918 November	Armistice, three months after Ludendorff told the Emperor that the war must be ended because the German army could not win: The Emperor abdicated; a republic was proclaimed; and the Socialists ruled as the majority party.
1919	The Spartacist Revolt in Berlin was led by the revolutionary left of Rosa Luxemburg and Karl Liebknecht. Contrary to their expectations, there was no spontaneous mass support for their revolt. Both were murdered by the arresting authorities.
1919 February	The Weimar Assembly, under threat of invasion, accepted the Versailles Treaty. The ruling majority Socialists and liberals were immediately denounced as traitors by traditional conservatives and the radical right from Hindenburg to Hitler.
1922–1924	Rabid inflation, and spiraling political assassinations by the right.
1923	The French invaded and occupied the Ruhr when the German government defaulted on absurdly high reparations payments.
1923 November 8–11	The so-called "Beer-Hall *Putsch*" of Ludendorff and Hitler: This attempt to overthrow the Bavarian government by force was a failure. For their treason, Hitler was jailed for less than a year and Ludendorff was unpunished. *Mein Kamf* was written by Hitler during his prison sentence.
1923–1929	The Stresemann period of relative accommodation with the West and partial fulfillment of the the terms of the Versailles Treaty: Stresemann

	died in 1929. His death and the (later) coming of the Depression pushed Germany to the right.
1930 March	Amid ever-increasing street violence between left and right, and the inability of the conservative nationalists to gain parliamentary majorities, Weimar democracy ended and Bruening ruled by emergency decree through Hindenburg's presidential authority.
1930 September 14	*Reichstag* elections: Hitler's National Socialist party became a national force with a jump from 12 to 107 seats. The middle parties lost heavily and the left remained strong—143 seats for the Socialists, 77 for the Communists. All this, be it noted, before the Depression was strongly felt.
1932	The full onslaught of the Depression was felt as 6 million were unemployed.
1932	Presidential election: Political polarization increased as Hindenburg received 18 million votes, Hitler 11 million, and Thaelmann (Communist) nearly 5 million. Hindenburg won the runoff against Hitler.
1932 May	Bruening resigned when Hindenburg refused to consider a moderate land reform in East Prussia. Franz von Papen, traditional autocratic reactionary and admirer of the feudal ethic, formed a "Cabinet of barons."
1932 June 16	The Government ended the ban on Nazi Street violence.
1932 July 20	A *Coup d'etat* in Prussia as von Papen purged Socialists and liberals from the government.
1932 December 2	Hitler refused a conditional appointment as Chancellor and General Kurt von Schleicher was appointed the head of government. His attempt to reconcile liberal elements with rightist rule made him unacceptable to the traditional groups around Hindenburg. On January 28th Schleicher resigned.

1933 January 30	Hitler was appointed Chancellor on his terms. He presided over a Cabinet of Nazis, Nationalists, and Conservatives.
1933 February 27	In the midst of Hitler's last election campaign but one, the *Reichstag* fire helped persuade some that only Hitler stood between them and the "international communist conspiracy."
1933 March 5	Election returns gave the Nazis and their aristocratic and big business allies 340 seats; the left gained 201 seats.
1933 March 23	The Enabling Act was passed giving full dictatorial powers to Hitler. All parties, excluding the Socialists and the outlawed Communists, voted in favor of it.
1933–1937	The totalitarianization of Germany: local governments were deprived of power, the civil service was purged of liberals and Jews, the judicial system was purged, rival parties were forbidden, Jewish businesses were liquidated, the Nuremberg laws defining "Jewishness" and providing appropriate punishments were passed, and concentrations camps were established. Culture, propaganda, the press, and the trade unions were placed under total controls. Autarchy, rearmament, and full employment became the goals of the regime, as Hitler prepared for his conquest of the East.
1933 October 14	Germany withdrew from the Disarmement Conference and the League of Nations.
1934 August	Hindenburg died, and in the presidential elections there was an 88 percent affirmative vote for Hitler. Representatives from the army, the landowners, and industry agreed that Hitler might rule alone, especially because, in June, he had purged his own left-wing.
1935 March 16	Hitler denounced the disarmament clause of the Treaty of Versailles.
1936 March 17	Germany occupied the Rhineland.

1936 October 27	The Berlin-Rome Axis.
1936 November 17	German-Japanese Pact.
1936 November 18	Hitler recognized Franco and sent aid.
1938 March	The Germans invaded and annexed Austria.
1939 March	The Germans occupied Bohemia, Moravia, and Memel.
1939 August	The Nazi-Soviet Pact, which cleared the way for Hitler and Stalin's mutual invasion of Poland.
1939 September 1	Hitler invaded Poland.
1939 September 3	England and France declared war on Germany.
1941	By this year, the Germans had conquered Poland, Denmark, Norway, the Netherlands, Belgium, and France; they had thrown the British army into the sea, and invaded Rumania, Greece, and Yugoslavia.
1941 June 22	Hitler invaded Russia.
1943 February 2	The conclusion of the most important battle of World War II, the battle of Stalingrad: Twenty-two German Divisions capitulated.
1943 May	The Germans surrendered in Africa.
1943 July 10	Italy was invaded by Anglo-American forces.
1944 June 6	The Normandy coast of France was invaded by the Western Allied Forces.
1944 July/August	The Germans were driven out of Russia by the Red army as it swept into Eastern Europe.

1944 July 20	A small group of high army officers attempted to assassinate Hitler.
1945 January	The Russians entered Germany in East Prussia. Warsaw fell.
1945 April	Hitler committed suicide.
1945	The German army in Italy surrendered.
1945 May 1	The Russians took Berlin.
1945 May 7	The German army leaders signed the terms of surrender.

HUNGARY

1918	Defeated in World War I: The Treaty of Trianon reduced Hungary's territory and population by one-third, and put three million Hungarians under foreign rule.
1918	The Hungarian Parliament declared its independence from Austria.
1918 October	Count Károlyi was made head of government after a bloodless revolution installed a Republic and removed the King.
1919 March	Károlyi, a liberal, resigned to protest the assignment of Hungarian territory to Rumania.
1919 March	A Socialist and Communist coalition government was formed, and was soon replaced by Béla Kun's Communist dictatorship—he promised, with Russian aid, to regain Hungary's lost territories. Hungary went to war with Czechoslovakia and Rumania.
1919 August 1	Béla Kun fled as the Rumanians, with encouragement of allies, advanced. Admiral Horthy and his (fascistic) anti-Bolshevik Committees retook Hungary and commenced a bloody white terror against Communists, Socialists, and Jews.

1920 March 23	Horthy was declared Regent and Head of State, and he proclaimed Hungary a monarchy. The Treaty of Trianon was signed in June.
1921–1931	The government, under Horthy, of Count Stephen Bethlen: Royalist and Fascist attempts at revolution were put down. The traditional conservative landed aristocracy ruled through Horthy and Bethlen. Universal suffrage was abolished.
1930s	Fascistic groups rose with the onset of the Depression. Among others, there were the Hungarian National Socialist Agricultural Laborers and Workers party; the Hungarian Hitlerite Group; the Hungarian National Socialist People's party; the Scythe Cross; and, in 1931, the most important of all, The Arrow Cross Hungarist movement and party under Ferenc Szálasi (1897–1944).
1932	The Great Depression put in power Gyula Gömbös (1886–1936), an admirer of Hitler and Mussolini and an outspoken Fascist. He replaced Count Bethlen and, forgetting his earlier calls for land reform, pursued the goals of unity with Italy and Germany in pursuit of Hungary's lost territories by war. He was well controlled by Horthy who insisted that Gömbös drop his leftism.
1933	Hitler's seizure of power led to a strong increase in Hungary of Fascist agitation. Gömbös visited Berlin and Rome. Many Hungarian aristocrats gave financial aid to fascistic movements, and the army was heavily infiltrated.
1936	Gömbös died of natural causes. He was succeeded by Daranyi.
1937 March 5	Ferenc Szálasi was arrested and punished because the government's traditional conservative landowners feared his agitation for land reform.
1937 October	Under Szálasi's leadership, various Hungarian National Socialist groups united and gained heavy German subsidies.

1938 February	Szálasi was arrested again by the ruling conservatives.
1938 May 13	A new cabinet was formed by Béla Imredy.
1938 November	As payment for cooperation with Germany, Hungary gained southern Slovakia.
1939 February	In one of the oddest events in the history of fascism, Premier Imredy resigned when, in the midst of an attempt to outdo competing Fascist leaders by anti-Semitic actions, it was discovered that his great-grandfather was Jewish! Count Paul Teleki formed a new government. (No improvement.) Hungary joined the anti-Communist Pact of Germany, Italy, and Japan.
1938–1939	Anti-Semitic laws were passed.
1939 February	Elections: Various fascist groups won 48 out of 259 seats—31 were won by the Arrow Cross. A significant victory but much aided by German funds.
1941	Hungary entered the war to aid the German invasion of Russia, but Horthy was extremely reluctant.
1944 March	The German occupation of Hungary.
1944 October	Horthy was arrested and interned by the Germans. Thousands of Hungarian Jews were transferred to Eichmann and death. Szálasi became the "National Leader" of Hungary with the support of many traditional conservative leaders. Szálasi carried out none of his "left" social reforms, but continued the general Fascist goal of the murder of anti-Fascists. Russian troops attacked Hungarian territory.
1945 April 4	The last German and Hungarian troops fled as the Russians entered Budapest. A Russian puppet government was set up.
1946	Szálasi was executed.

SPAIN

1873–1874	The First Spanish Republic was proclaimed.
1875–1885 December	The Republic was overthrown by generals who put in King Alfonso XII.
1876	A new Constitution established an apparent parliamentary government. The King, not the Cortés, ruled, however, and the Church increased its secular powers.
1890	Universal suffrage was reintroduced. Anarchist disturbances led to repressive legislation and executions. Throughout the 1890s, socialism, anarchism, and regionalism gained strength.
1898	The loss of the Spanish-American war and Cuba led to both a left and right radical reaction.
1902–1931	The reign of Alfonso XIII.
1909	As army power increased over the civilian population, the left protested both the sending of troops to Morocco, and the discrimination obvious in the military draft against the lower classes. A general strike, which spread rapidly, was declared at Barcelona—Priests and monks were murdered, convents were burned, and violent counterrepression was carried out.
1910–1913	The liberals were in power. Their Premier, Canalejas, was assassinated after moving legislation to weaken the secular powers of the Church. The conservatives gained power.
1914	Spain declared her neutrality in World War I. The war brought an upsurge of Spanish industry, and gave a boost to the forces of the left. This, in turn, stimulated more fear among landowners, army officers, and church officials.
1921	In Morocco, the Riffs inflicted a disastrous defeat on Spanish troops, and the right suppressed demands for an investigation.

1923 September 13	The *coup d'etat* of General Miguel Primo de Rivera: Liberals were imprisoned, the Cortés was suppressed, and a military dictatorship was imposed in response to the rising republican sentiment.
1924 November	General Miguel Primo de Rivera and the King visited Mussolini and (in 1926) signed a treaty of friendship.
1930 January	Primo de Rivera resigned in face of liberal, republican, socialist, and anarchist agitation.
1930	The Spanish Nationalist party was formed. Expressing ultraconservative ideas, the new party engaged in street violence against the left.
1931 April	Municipal elections gave an overwhelming victory to republicanism. King Alfonso left Spain.
1931 June	The elections to the Constituent Assembly were a great victory for Republicans and Socialists.
1931	Redondo Ortega, a right extremist leading a predominantly lower-middle class Fascist movement, joined with Ramiro Ledesma Ramos who had founded a small Spanish Fascist movement on the Nazi model. The joint organization was known as JONS.
1931 December	The new Constitution was adopted—with universal suffrage; a President chosen by popular vote (with no army officer or cleric eligible); and with the government given power to expropriate private property, nationalize utilities, and enforce the separation of church and state.
1932	The *Falange Española,* the most important Spanish Fascist organization, was founded by Jose Antonio Primo de Rivera, the son of the former military dictator of Spain and related to wealthy commercial families. Within a year, other radical right groups merged with the Falange. The Falange had 5000 members by 1934.
1932 August	General Sanjurjo attempted a coup from the right but failed.

1933 January 8	Anarchists and syndicalists rose in many cities.
1936 February 16	Elections: This was the last straw for the traditional rulers of Spain. The Popular Front of Republicans, syndicalists, Socialists, and Communists defeated the Front formed by the right-wing parties. Azãna formed a government, and was elected President of the Republic. Social reform, including attacks on the power of the church, landowners, and army was certain to be increased. The middle and upper-middle classes moved to the far right. The Falange was outlawed by the government.
1936 July 18	Led by General Francisco Franco, the army revolted in Morocco and Spain.
1937	The Falangists and Carlists became allies.
1939 January 26	Franco took Barcelona. England and France recognized his government.
1939 March 28	Madrid surrendered and the Civil War ended.
1939 September	Spain indicated her neutrality in World War II.

ENGLAND

1905–1914	Under the guidance of the Liberal Party the basic outlines of the modern welfare state were established. This provoked an ultraconservative counterreaction. The welfare state measures included the famous "soak the rich" People's Budget of 1909, various health and welfare measures, and the weakening of the power of the House of Lords.
1914 August 4	England entered World War I in response to the German invasion of Belgium and hostilities against France.
1918	A severe postwar economic crisis was caused by

	the human and material costs of the war, the increased world competition in industrial production, and the increasing independence of subject areas.
1919–1922	A Coalition government was created by the war leader, David Lloyd George. Two million were unemployed by 1921.
1923 November 15	Great gains were made by the Labor party. The Conservatives under Bonar Law and Stanley Baldwin, however, won and the Liberal party split. Labor gains provoked a radical conservative reaction among the Tories. The British Fascists were founded in 1923.
1924 January to November	The first Labor government was formed under Ramsay MacDonald. Fascistic groups supported by old-line Tories came into existence, though they were hardly as significant in numbers or wealth as their continental counterparts.
1924 October	A great electoral victory of the Conservatives over Labor, partly on the basis of forged "evidence" (The Zinoviev letter) which alleged that the Labor party was directly under the control of the "international Communist conspiracy."
1926	The great general strike in sympathy with the striking miners. Almost three million workers left their jobs. The upper classes (and fascistic groups) kept the essential services going. By November, the miners were forced to surrender unconditionally.
1926	General election: Labor won 288 seats to the Conservatives 260.
1929	Arnold Leese founded the Imperial Fascist League. He called for the murder of all Jews through gassing. In the late 1920s, Sir Oswald Mosley was still attempting to lead a splinter group of left laborites to a revolutionary transformation of Great Britain.
1931	A National Coalition Government was formed of the three major parties with MacDonald as

	Prime Minister. The Labor party expelled MacDonald and his supporters. The Coalition government was formed to meet the Depression crisis. It lasted until 1935. Great Britain abandoned the gold standard and other liberal economic principles as it adopted economic nationalism and neomercantilism.
1931	Mosley broke with the Labor party and founded the British Union of Fascists, after his return from a visit to Mussolini in Rome in 1932.
1934	The depth of the Depression and the height of Fascist influence. The famous Albert Hall meeting was attended by 10,000 Fascists. The violence employed by the Fascist shock troops at this meeting caused many sympathetic Tories to reject them as a possible defense against socialism. The success of Hitler also caused many Tories to suspect Mosley's group as being under German influence and "not really British."
1936	The death of George V, was followed by the accession of Edward VIII, his abdication, and the coronation of George VI.
1937 May	Neville Chamberlain became Prime Minister.
1938 September	The Munich Agreement: Chamberlain, hoping to pacify Hitler and gain time for Great Britain, agreed to yield the Sudetenland to the Germans. As Germany became once again the enemy, the influence of all fascistic groups, never great, sharply receded. Rearmament proceeded.
1939 September 3	War: Mosley and other Fascists were jailed.

THE FASCIST TRADITION

THE NATURE OF FASCISM

The Blackshirts Have What the Conservatives Need

—Headline, lead article, *Daily Mail,* 1934—written by A CONSERVATIVE M.P.

It is odd to find a study of such revolutionary and recent phenomena as fascism and national socialism included in a series presenting the major traditions of World Civilization. The layman, still numbed by the horror of the extermination camps and the deliberate slaughter of millions of innocents, inevitably looks upon Fascists and Nazis as the terrible and unique excrescenses of a single generation. Scholars as well have usually regarded the radical totalitarianism of Mussolini and Hitler as singular and transient responses to the radical social dislocations of the years between the two great wars. And perhaps because the Nazis have received the bulk of popular and scholarly attention, the radical right has too often been thought of as the exclusive product of those specifically German traditions which deviate from the norms of Western European historical development.

But the original and contemporaneous nature of

fascism has been, I think, much overemphasized.[1] Certainly there has been no fascist tradition if by that one means a continuous and long-term fascistic response to social change by powerful and established groups. Mussolini's words, "I am a reactionary and a revolutionary," are appropriate here. Fascism, after all, is a conservative social movement, however radical. As such, it is closely related to ideas, interests, and classes active in Western Civilization since the first great challenge to conservative values during the French Revolution of 1789. It is this relationship that has not been fully explored. It is fortunate, however, that few attempt any longer to explain the origins of fascism and national socialism by reference to the supposed unique and collective guilt of the German people, or the alleged demonic irrationalism of modern man, or the gangsterism of a handful of nihilistic leaders committed to power and power alone. But as yet not enough has been done to show how the radical right plays on the fears and represents the hopes of traditional conservatives. As I hope to show, the reactionary revolutionaries who seized power in Italy and Germany did so largely because they gained power and support from older conservative classes, and prestige from a previously established conservative intellectual tradition.

It would be wrong to blur the important and real distinctions between older conservative classes and ideas, and the terroristic extremists of European fascism. But such differences have been overstressed. Certainly it is absurd and foolish to regard a Bismarck as a precursor of fascism.

[1] For the sake of convenience, I will use the term "fascism" to refer to the general social movement of right-wing revolutionary conservatism in Europe, reserving the term "Fascism" (capitalized) to designate any political party calling itself such (as in Italy and Britain). Similarly, the terms "Nazi" and "National Socialism" will refer solely to the German phenomenon or groups calling themselves by these names elsewhere, while "nazi" and "national socialism" (lower case) will be used to refer to any movement sharing their German counterpart's characteristics wherever they appear.

Nor do I wish to add my name to that long list of misguided scholars who have ignored the diverse subtleties and sophisticated ambiguities of the great conservative intellectuals and have placed them among the ranks of so-called fascist "precursors"—as has been done with Fichte, Carlyle, Hegel, and Nietzsche, for example. It is true, of course, that Nazi propagandists liked to present their movement as the direct heir of a Frederick the Great, a Bismarck, or a Nietzsche; but this could be done only by arbitrary selection, simple distortion, or outright falsehood.

Intellectual historians have confused the issue by their outmoded method of regarding a handful of leading theorists as the major carriers or representatives of the conservative (or liberal, or socialist, etc.) intellectual tradition. Such esoteric and brilliant thinkers as Fichte and Nietzsche have no real influence on large groups or classes of men, and thus no direct influence on that great abstraction we call history. They are altogether too complicated and subtle to be heard beyond a few. Consequently, massive social movements are not to be understood unless one considers the collective, crude, and simple attitudes and opinions of sizable social groups and classes. As we shall see, the Fascists and Nazis succeeded in part because they echoed the values and interests not of a handful of conservative intellectuals, but of aristocratic landowners, military leaders, reactionary industrialists, small shopkeepers, and small-holding peasantry. I am well aware that one cannot thereby accuse such groups of advocating unlimited terror, extermination camps, and World War II. For men making political choices do not usually will or even know all the indirect consequences of achieving what they want. And, also, the starkly narrow limits of alternative political choices actually open to social groups defending their interests under great threat is a factor students of politics as well as intellectual historians cannot afford to overlook.

And this is my major point: The radical right thrives in societies where older but still powerful conservative classes are threatened by rapid and modernizing social change; change which creates or gives strength to liberal and radical classes and groups antagonistic toward "the old ways." Thus, in the twentieth century, the minority of revolutionary conservatives always present in modern Europe became the needed counterreaction and the defenders of conservatism *in extremus*. Any study of fascism which centers too narrowly on the Fascists and Nazis alone may miss the true significance of right-wing extremism. For without necessarily becoming party members or accepting the entire range of party principles themselves, aristocratic landlords, army officers, government and civil service officials, and important industrialists in Italy and Germany helped bring Fascists and Nazis to power. In doing so, after the end of World War I, they were motivated by the fear that loss of their power, prestige, wealth, and values would shortly follow the new participation of the masses in full-fledged parliamentary democracy. The radical right was to constitute the last line of defense against the mounting liberal and radical agitation for land reform, social welfare measures, demilitarization, higher wages, and the socialization of the means of production. War, inflation, and the Great Depression certainly polarized social attitudes into extremes of left and right and opened vast opportunities to the radical right; but the basic social conflict was as old as the rise of liberalism.

Too often scholars have stressed the ideological and political differences between old conservatives and new ultraconservatives but have failed to perceive how willing the respectable conservatives have been to trade these differences with their own ultraright wing in order to prevent the victory of liberalism and radicalism and the triumph of mass democracy. The well-known slogan so often heard among the French aristocrats and businessmen in 1935 tells the story: "Better Hitler than Leon Blum." And Blum, be it noted, though ostensibly a Socialist, threatened in fact only a French version of the "New Deal." Many of the most important European industrialists shared this attitude, of course; yet the familiar Marxist formula must be discarded. Fascism was not the "last gasp of monopoly capitalism." If anything, it was the last gasp of conservatism.

Other reasons have convinced many able scholars, however, that fascism is not primarily a conservative movement. As they point out, Fascists and Nazis received massive electoral support from large sections of what are normally held to be the middle and lower-middle classes: self-employed small businessmen, artisans, shopkeepers, clerical white-collar workers, lower civil servants, peasants, impoverished gentry, domestics, and pensioners. It should be remembered, however, that in general such supporters of fascism insofar as they were liberal, were so only in the sense, say, that members of the John Birch Society are liberal; i.e., they stood for the values of early nineteenth-century liberalism. Such ossified liberalism is starkly conservative in our time. It opposes representative democracy, trade-unionism, and the social legislation of the modern neoliberal welfare state; and it supports a rigid defense of the rights of private property regardless of social cost. Often caught between the competitive drive of big business and the organizing drive of trade union radicalism, these middle and lower-middle class groups were made desperate by the traumatic experiences of war, inflation, and depression, as well as by the overwhelming status anxieties which followed. And they felt even more threatened than the traditional conservatives by the steady advance and future prospects of welfare state liberalism and working class agitation. To both upper and middle class conservatives, Mussolini and Hitler offered, through street violence and totalitarian controls, the surest means of halting both international "Jewish" liberalism and trade union "bolshevism."

German and Italian experience seems to suggest that, although fascistic movements are to be found in all modern countries, fascism does not thrive unless brought to power, directly or indirectly, by a supportive alliance of preliberal power elites (semifeudal or aristocratic), reactionary industrialists, and elements of the socially frustrated lower-middle class. Such an alliance, given the acute social conflicts generated by total war and economic chaos, easily if not deliberately falls victim to the most violent enemies of liberalism and radicalism—the extremists on the right.

Once in power, however, Fascists and Nazis were unwilling to act as simple lackeys of those interests which brought them to office. Indeed, they could not do so. Fascism cannot remain in control if it acts like previous despotisms or mere conservative coalition governments—governments such as those of a Franco, a Pilsudski, or a Horthy. Fascism is not traditional but revolutionary conservatism; and fascists must inaugurate unique, sweeping, and dynamic policies of systematic terror and total control over all areas of national life. For they come to power in societies where the developing historical forces of liberalism and radicalism have generated a mortal challenge to upper and lower class conservatives. Only where modernism (with all that that implies) has gained few social footholds, can traditional autocrats control liberalism and leftism with relative ease. The casual, sporadic, and noninstitutionalized violence of the old-fashioned despot can prevail only in an "underdeveloped" society where the liberal thrust is enfeebled by the continued existence of preliberal elites and social structures, as in Spain and Hungary. In such societies, traditional conservatives themselves may very well reject as dangerous and unnecessary the dynamic fascist totalitarian institutionalization of terror and social controls.

It is not yet understood why Fascists and Nazis followed an extremist and unprecedented policy of aggressive imperialism. Traditional despotisms have usually been militarist and, when powerful, expansive. But the radical right in power conquered and exploited subject peoples with a nightmarish ruthlessness that indicates a qualitative difference. As I have sought to indicate in the following pages, the conquest and total exploitation of subject peoples was, for Nazis and Fascists, an utter necessity. Otherwise, they were likely to fall victim to the very social dislocations which brought them to power, and to the internal tensions created by their totalitarian rule. When Hitler and Mussolini militarized the culture, economy, and outlook of their people, they were expressing a general tendency of the radical right everywhere to substitute military aggression and internal force for those progressive social reforms which could only strengthen the hands of their liberal and radical opponents. Since the mid-nineteenth century, militant nationalism had been the policy of conservative politics. But here too, the revolutionary reactionaries carried conservative policies to qualitatively new extremes. Even anti-Semitism, so predominant among Central and Eastern European fascists, was not simply arbitrary "scapegoatism" but an attempt to purge the nation of just those groups which, especially in Central and Eastern Europe, represented outstandingly liberal professions and radical views. In short, both terror at home and terror abroad, under fascism, were attempts to resolve political, economic, and social problems without the sacrifice of conservative and reactionary values.

I have presented general principles first in order to give the reader some thematic guidance through the following chapters. Inevitably, such a brief description of a general theory of fascism cannot do justice to the wealth of available facts; and it must seem rigid, abstract, and question-begging. In the following pages I hope to present the evidence and analysis necessary to adequately modify and illustrate what may seem arbitrary and unsatisfying in these first few pages.

The ensuing chapters are arranged in the following sequence. First, a general discussion of fascist ideology with emphasis on its relationship to earlier conservative ideas. Subsequent chapters turn to the Fascist and Nazi seizure of power, with special reference to those groups and classes which supported the radical right and their reasons for doing so. The failure of a social movement in a particular cultural and political environment often reveals as much as its success. Therefore, I have included special sections on the failure of fascism in a liberal Western nation—England—and its failure in two "underdeveloped" European nations dominated by traditional conservatism—Spain and Hungary. As with Italy and Germany, I have tried to show what historical conditions and social tensions seem to make a society vulnerable to revolutionary conservatism. Finally, returning to Italy and Germany, I have analyzed the social policies and totalitarian structure of fascism in power, and the reason for its destructive urge to total war and imperialism.

THE IDEOLOGY OF THE RADICAL RIGHT

The main plank in the National Socialist program is to abolish the liberal concept of the individual and the Marxist concept of humanity, and to substitute for them the Volk *community, rooted in the soil and united by the bond of its common blood.*
—ADOLPH HITLER, 1937

Fascists and National Socialists push many traditional conservative ideas to radical and vulgar extremes, but they do not abandon them. As "new" conservatives they do not want to be taken for mere defenders of the old reactionary elite, and insist endlessly that their movement is dynamic, unique, and, above all, modern. Those who write the history of social movements must be careful, however, not to take ideological statements at face value. "New" conservatives must disguise the ancient lineage of their ideas if only because a social movement that defends established interests within a mass democracy must generate a mass appeal. Because of this, most of the current generalizations about the ideology of the radical right are misleading. We are told, for example, that fascists have no program, that they are nihilistic opportunists who select from the body of their self-contradictory ideas just those which will clear the immediate obstacles on the road to power. Fascism has also been called a demonic outburst of the irrational in modern man. Until recently, fascism, as National Socialism, has been thought a transient and peculiarly Germanic response to the particular social dislocations of the interwar years. Comparisons are in order. The ideology which won power in Italy and Germany, came close to power in Rumania, Spain, Hungary, and Austria, and was present, though weak, in England, France, Belgium, Holland, and Finland. As we have good reason to know in the United States, right-wing extremism finds supporters even during times of affluence and relative social stability. As for fascism's alleged "irrationality," it is, in reality, not so much a revolt against reason as a revolt against liberalism which liberals have found unreasonable. Like it or not, fascist ideology is international in scope, fairly self-consistent, and presents a rational, i.e., workable, if frightening, set of political, social, and economic alternatives to the reigning liberalism of the West.[1]

As a revolutionary form of nineteenth-century conservatism, right-wing extremism won conscious expression as ideology with liberalism's first great triumphs in the

[1] It would be a distortion of the unity of the ideology of the radical right if I were to attempt to credit each idea in the following pages to any one ideologist. Let me merely list here the most important names: Hitler and Mussolini, of course, but also: Alfredo Rocco and Giovanni Gentile (Italy), Georges Valois and Marcel Déat (France), Sir Oswald Mosley and Arnold Leese (England), H. S. Chamberlain and Alfred Rosenberg (Germany), José Antonio Primo de Rivera (Spain), Cornelius Zelea Codreanu (Rumania), Ferenc Szálasi (Hungary), and Léon Degrelle (Belgium).

French Revolution of 1789. The central organizing metaphor of nineteenth-century conservative thought was that of the "organic" or "corporate" state. Defending themselves against an increasingly victorious liberal establishment, conservatives throughout the nineteenth century attacked the constitutional, democratic, and pragmatic "interest" state. Like the fascists later, conservatives projected the counter-image of an organic *Volk* community, loyal to traditional ways, and guided by an elite capable of "intuiting" the true national spirit and needs of the masses. Both old and new conservatives condemned natural-rights individualism as an ideology which had destroyed true communal unity and had ennobled the utilitarian calculus of merely private or class selfishness. The state, they insisted, is a complex organism with each part playing a vital role in the maintenance of a natural harmony of functions. Anarchy is courted by those who demand abstract individual freedom, unlimited upward mobility, or social equality rather than communal responsibilities to "one's station and its duties." Fascists ignored their conservative predecessors in order to claim a new and revolutionary approach to politics. But those exiled nobles who first fled the French Revolution of 1789 would have recognized a kindred spirit in twentieth-century fascism, for it was a projection of the counterrevolutionary hopes of their own radical right wing.

Traditionally, the political ideal of the organic state was related to philosophical idealism and conservative nationalism. Conservatives and fascists after them accused liberals and leftists of a crass and demeaning concern with the mere material welfare of the individual. Liberalism, conservatives had argued throughout the nineteenth century, held a mechanistic or "atomistic" view of the state and society, a view which reduced both to mere collective nouns or inconvenient fictions. Bourgeois shopkeepers, as fascists alleged later, would hardly sacrifice themselves to the noble ideal of the nation. The more philosophically inclined fascist intellectuals (a Gentile, a Déat, a Codreanu, or a Rocco) put it so: Beyond the brute surface appearance of material phenomena, there exists an immutable and eternal realm of which the nation is an immediate and intrinsic expression. From Codreanu, the Rumanian peasant-mystic and fascist leader, to the sophisticated and perhaps ghost-written words of Mussolini, a crude philosophical idealism was the norm. Thus Mussolini wrote:

> Fascism is a religious belief in which man is seen in imminent relationship with a superior and objective will that transcends the particular individual and raises him to conscious membership in a spiritual society.

Conservative idealists made similar statements again and again in the nineteenth century, from the Hegelians of the right to the Objective Idealists and primitive spiritualists at the end of the century. Typically the radical right pushed older ideas to revolutionary extremes. As opposed to the alleged materialistic individualism of liberalism, fascists insisted on the primacy of the collective—whether tribe, community, or nation. Thus Mussolini once again:

> We want a life in which the individual, through the sacrifice of his own private interests, through death itself, realizes that complete spiritual existence in which lies his value as a man.

Fascist ideologists agreed with their conservative predecessors that liberals, radicals, and socialists were antihistorical. Allegedly, they ignored the prior claims of those national institutions and customs won by the sweat and blood of past generations. They worked only for the transient animal needs of their contemporary generation. Throughout fascist ideology there runs a strain of glowing references to an imagined primal, barbaric peasant-warrior tribalism—whether in the Turanianism of Hungarian fascism, or the teutonic founding chieftains of Nordic national socialism. To replace the sophisticated and urbane spirit of liberal internationalism, Fascists and Nazis preached the instinctual and single-minded unity of race, the passion of heroic sacrifice for the tribe, and the militant aggression of the *Volk*. Once again Mussolini, this time speaking, appropriately enough, to the brave Italian shock troops of World War I: "Our myth is the nation; our myth is the greatness of the nation."

Since the middle of the nineteenth century, conservatives had appealed to national unity in order to discredit the criticism of social reformists. Certainly conservatives often directed organic state concepts against capitalists, often arguing, for example, that the feudal lord had shown a true paternal regard for his peasantry, a regard that put modern factory owners to shame. Similarly, European fascists often demanded help for the workers; and many youthful idealists and unemployed workers joined the ultraright to help enforce the *socialism* of national socialism. They were to be disillusioned. In the rise to power of Fascists and Nazis, the need to wean the masses from the left was cancelled out by the need for financial aid from industrialists. But simple hypocrisy is hardly a complete explanation. The true enemy for old and new conservatives alike was *modern* liberalism. This is obscured by the right's pose as the only serious anti-Communist movement, and its related claim that there are few if any important differences between the various ideologies to their left. Tactical advantages, of course, are to be had by those who can successfully label their opponents "unconscious or conscious agents of the Communist conspiracy." Nevertheless, the most sophisticated and sincere ideologists of the radical right state again and again: Those who accept the liberal premise that politics are primarily concerned with the social welfare of the individual, will, depending on social conditions, easily and inevitably range the gamut from liberalism through socialism to bolshevism. Thus the ultraright joined the old reactionaries of Europe, who without ideological trappings, simply labeled moderate land reform and progressive tax policies as outright bolshevism.

"Democracy," Hitler insisted, "is nothing other than the systematic cultivation of human failure." The thought is old and familiar, and it expresses with contempt conservative fears aroused by the gradual inclusion of the masses in Western political life. Fascist ideologists (often misusing the ideas of a Carlyle or a Nietzsche even when they did not misrepresent them) condemned liberalism and socialism on the grounds that they pandered to the mediocrity of the faceless herd and denied the creative will and force of the natural aristocracy. Restating some of the conservative neoidealism of the turn of the century, the European radical right accused liberals and Marxists alike of holding an ignoble view of man—a view of man as a mere puppet of vast, impersonal, and unsensed material forces. In the fascist view, the great system builders of nineteenth-century Europe ignored man's will, conscious purpose, and intellect by virtue of their essentially theological belief in progressive systems of automatically self-regulating natural law. Whatever else divided Karl Marx, Adam Smith, or Herbert Spencer, fascist intellectuals argued, they were united by the idea that great social and historical transformations are brought about by millions of petty decisions made by self-centered masses reacting in reflex patterns brought about by the crass stimuli of the market place. It was this that Mussolini, for example, had in mind when he said that Fascism has no program but is purpose, will, and heroic act.

Correspondingly, Fascist intellectuals were often fascinated by the antidemocratic theories of the elite, theories propagated by men like Georges Sorel and Vilfredo Pareto—both were especially singled out by Mussolini. Pareto taught a generation to see politics, especially the politics of mass democracies, as nothing more than a simple conflict among narrow power-elites who cloaked their private interests in the rhetoric of idealism but were not animated by any higher sense of responsibility to people or principles. Where parliamentary liberalism was in fact no more than the defense of property by a small oligarchy —as in Italy, Spain, Rumania, and Hungary—these theories offered young bourgeois intellectuals respectable, intellectually conservative, and authoritarian alternatives to the liberal establishment. It must be remembered that in relatively underdeveloped nations liberalism appears as little more than the defense of the privileges of the owning classes. And that there fascists found, perhaps paradoxically, at once a means of condemning the ruling oligarchy and of justifying their own cult of force and will to power. True leadership, even true democracy, fascists argued, exists only where the *Volk*, by mass acclamation, thrust up a *Volk* leader who intuits their real needs and national spirit and who forges the *Volk* into a collective unity capable of performing great, violent, and self-sacrificial acts. There is some evidence that Mussolini, late in life, lamented his own betrayal of this Fascist ideal; for, as he well knew, his regime defended the crass interests of the landowning and business classes even as it propagated the myth of the rule of an heroic elite (an elite allegedly beyond all crass materialism and class selfishness).

Some scholars argue against classifying fascism as ultraconservative because of its powerful strain of anticapitalist ideas. This argument, however, overlooks the existence of a full-blown, lower-middle class, anticapitalist ideology which was as old as capitalism itself, and had been embodied in the traditional conservative theories of the organic state. The guildsmen, artisans, small peasants, and marginal traders of Southern, Central, and Eastern Europe feared the introduction of free-enterprise capitalism from the beginning of the industrialism of Europe. It threatened the remnants of their highly protective guild system, with its market agreements; price, wage, and quality controls; and regulations limiting entrance into the trades. Throughout Europe, wherever industrial capitalism spread, guildmasters, small shopkeepers, and artisans in the villages fought a desperate and losing battle against free markets, unlimited mass production, and the uncontrolled expansion of liberal capitalism. The ideology of this much-ignored fight of the old order against the new is to be found in the pamphlets, journals, and proceedings of many guild congresses, small businessmen's associations, and tradesmen's groups, as well as in numerous appeals intended to persuade local and national government to transform guild monopolies into law and severely restrict free enterprise. Throughout the nineteenth century, consequently, capitalism was viewed by artisans, small businessmen, and small traders much as Fascist ideologists, searching for lower-middle class support, have viewed it in our time. These groups saw capitalism as an alien, un-German, international, even "Jewish" revolutionary force which threatened to remove the traditional, Germanic, and Christian limits to the ruthless competitive search for profit. Long before Hitler, Codreanu, or Szálasi, there were widespread anti-Semitic and ultranationalistic *Bunds* formed among craftsmen and artisans to protect German workers from "Jewish" competition, as well as numerous groups formed among the small farmers, who blamed their economic troubles on Jewish cattle dealers, innkeepers, and mortgage holders. Indeed, in Central and Eastern Europe the nineteenth century had seen anti-Semitic riots espoused by these groups and led by demagogues who, in a later day, would have been called fascists.

Conservative intellectuals, economists, and social theorists in Central, Southern, and Eastern Europe had never accepted what they regarded as the a-historical rigidities of *laissez faire* economic individualism. Many conservatives hoped to find what they called a "third way" which would avoid the alleged heartless competitive egoism of liberal capitalism as well as the supposed soulless materialism and class antagonisms generated by Marxist socialism. The term "national socialism" was used before the advent of Nazis and Fascists by advocates of political controls for guided economic growth and paternalistic programs for social welfare. The "national socialism" concept, although not peculiar to fascism, enabled ideologists of the radical right to relate to an older nonliberal tradition—which, in Germany, for example, stretched from Frederick the Great to Bismarck and has been variously termed *Prussian, national,* or *conservative socialism.* The ideologists and political activists Gottfried Feder and Gregor and Otto Strasser (often called "left" Nazis), along with Hitler, were able to develop and direct this traditional but latent anticapitalism into an attack against what they called "destructive-Jewish-liberal-international finance-capitalism," and its alleged internal branches, the Jewish-owned department stores, mammoth trading outlets, and retail corporations. These were the enterprises which most often competed directly with those lower-middle class, self-employed businessmen who gave so many votes to the Nazis and European fascists. The European radical right promised to protect small businessmen from "destructive" competition by regulation and subsidy. Hitler, meanwhile, assured his industrialist backers that good, constructive, Teutonic industrial capital would have its profits and power guaranteed through autarchy and German market monopolies as Germany's armed might increased. This famous and false distinction between "destructive" and "constructive" capitalism, enabled the Nazis to channel the anticapitalism of the lower-middle class into ultranationalism, militarism, and anti-Semitism. Nothing shows Hitler's intellectual and political sensitivity better than this ideological gambit. By it he assured his important backers in industry that Nazi anticapitalism was really anti-Semitism; and he diverted the lower-middle class from seeking redress for their grievances in left radicalism and concrete economic reform.

Consequently, the radical right in Germany organized its ultraconservative ideas around a limitless and murderous anti-Semitic racial nationalism. This was possible primarily because the Jews of Central and Eastern Europe were overrepresented in just those urban, professional, cultural, and commercial classes which are usually the chief support of liberalism and radicalism.[2] Conservatism and anti-Semitism had been allied since at least those days when Napoleon forced some of the practices of revolutionary liberalism east of the Rhine. Those lesser gentry who, during the Prussian reform era, freed serfs, granted self-government to municipalities, introduced social mobility,

[2] Italian Fascists were not anti-Semitic or racial nationalists (though certainly ultranationalistic) and passed no anti-Semitic laws until late in the 1930s, and then only under German pressure. Italian historical development made it hardly possible to equate the urban, liberal, and modern spirit—almost an Italian invention!—with alien "races."

and agitated for a constitution, were denounced by aristocratic spokesmen. These spokesmen called for the defense of the ancient "Germanic-Christian social order" against the vile and despotic anarchy of such "Jewish-French and liberal" principles. When Bismarck unified Germany with the might of reactionary Prussia, German nationalism became conservative through and through, and racist precisely because it was conservative. The famous imperialistic and ultrapatriotic Pan-German society, for example, was directed by leading aristocrats, industrialists, and army officers and found its main support among white-collar workers and small businessmen. One of its most important leaders, and for a while Hitler's chief political rival, was Alfred Hugenberg, a former Director of Krupp, who hoped for a German rebirth through the expulsion of the Jews and the aggressive expansion of Germany to the east. The German Conservative party (DNVP), an embattled bastion of far rightist sentiment after 1918, was also *the* status party for aristocrats, gentry, upper civil servants, and social-climbing industrialists. Heinrich Class, the leader of the Conservative party at one time, might easily have written *Mein Kampf* in all essentials. The most prestigious veterans' organization, the *Stahlhelm*—a veritable club for upper and middle class elites—shared ideas with the radical right and put together the same combination of anti-Semitism and militaristic imperialism. Furthermore, neither conservative nor Nazi racial nationalism was limited to anti-Semitism. Long before Hitler spoke with murderous intent of the "subhuman" Slavic masses, traditional conservatives—both reactionary and moderate—thought it Germany's mission to force Teutonic civilization on the hapless Slavs. To most Germans, for that matter, the Slavs had demonstrated their racial inferiority by their lack of historical and cultural achievements. In short, the radical right found a ready-made alliance between racism and conservatism which it had only to exploit.

In Central, Eastern, and Southern Europe, semifeudal conservative classes were strong and, with the help of their radical right wing, had kept alive a powerful counterethic to liberal modernism. But, wherever liberalism and its institutions dominated (as in England and France) nationalism and conservatism could not be equated, and the radical right could hardly claim a monopoly on patriotism. Intellectually, the radical right shared the ancient hostility of aristocracy, gentry, and peasantry toward the city and its urbane and liberal culture. Fascist ideologists, like their conservative predecessors, attacked the city as the home of a traditionless, sterile, and radical spirit of nihilistic tolerance, a place of quick gain without corresponding service, and extreme moral decay. (The rallying cry, be it noted, of the radical right in America today.) Both Mussolini and Hitler preferred the stolid, national ways of the countryside, and looked upon the city as a natural culture for the germs of the liberal, radical, and Bolshevik plague threatening the ancient decency of the *Volk*. It was a French fascist who, upon visiting Paris, cried out in alarm: "Who are these foreigners who rule us?" The Hungarian radical right, led by the Magyar aristocracy, purged Budapest in the White Terror of 1920 as "the sinful city"—and shot Jews out of hand.

The young Hitler accurately mirrored the radical right's low tolerance for variety and ambiguity when he harangued against the mixed nationalities, languages, and life-styles of cosmopolitan Vienna. For the German and Austrian radical right, Vienna was the city which above all was given over to moral degeneracy and racial desecration. It was no accident that the larger the city the smaller the Nazi vote, or that the "ideal-typical" radical right voter throughout Central and Eastern Europe dwelled in village or farming community. To counter their caricature of the rootless and revolutionary city proletariat, the old and new right projected another caricature: the sturdy, honest, manly peasant-warrior, who, living close to his native soil, embodies all the truly national virtues and traditions. Conservatives and ultraconservatives thus gained the inestimable advantage which comes to any old guard when it can plausibly label liberalism and radicalism as alien and unpatriotic intrusions from abroad. Where the industrial city was a late development—as in Eastern Europe—neofeudalism and fascism were easily blended. Since the French Revolution, the Central European peasantry had been praised by conservatives for its alleged willingness to place duties before rights, and perform its humble functions within the organic society. Large landowners and well-off peasants found here a set of values to oppose the rising expectations of the exploited and land-hungry peasant proletariat. Thus, as with the lower-middle class in general, the urge for economic and social reform was diverted toward a vicious anti-Semitism. In Rumania, for example, the peasant fascist leader Codreanu wanted to destroy the Jews because, he argued, they were an alien, urbanized, and un-Rumanian class, intervening disruptively between the truly Rumanian orders of gentry and peasantry.

Enough has been said, perhaps, so that Hitler's *Mein Kampf* will not be taken as either original, irrational, or even peculiarly Germanic. In *Mein Kampf*, Hitler translated the sophisticated ideas of aristocratic conservatism into the vulgar language of German lower-middle class culture. He was hardly the first to do so, and he did it in the way others had done in the last decades of the nineteenth century: He pushed to violent extremes a conspiracy theory of history. This conspiracy theory had been in existence ever since

Metternich had blamed the Protestant Reformation on a few arrogant individuals, and fleeing aristocrats had blamed the French Revolution on a Masonic plot. Hitler's greatest intellectual achievement was to unite by this means all classes and groups threatened by the steady advance of liberalism, radicalism, and socialism. This political function of Hitler's conspiracy theory explains why millions could accept its alleged irrationality. Rather than acquiesce in the downfall of one's own class or group as the necessary consequence of general social and economic progress—or simply change generated by vast political, economic, and intellectual forces—the conspiracy theory enabled one to brand liberalism and socialism as the hypocritical emanations of a handful of international plotters. From Hitler and countless others, embattled conservatives heard that their troubles were brought about by an international Jewish-Liberal-Bolshevik conspiracy which hid its villainous attack on Nordic values behind such deceptive and progressive-sounding abstractions as democracy, social justice, peace, humanitarianism, and other non-Aryan definitions of progress. With typical radical right techniques, Hitler effectively sidestepped all concrete and complex analyses of social issues, intimidated those who wrestled with the problem of mass industrial societies, and rescued conservative values from the liberal onslaught. In short, with *Mein Kampf* Hitler was able to harness the legitimate fears and grievances of conservatives to a vast and deadly Nazi counter-conspiracy against the spontaneous forces of social change in industrial societies.

Neither the conservatives nor the general public in Germany could accept, for example, the defeat of the German armies in World War I: a defeat for which, even before Hitler's *Mein Kampf*, Germans held the collapse of the home front in 1918 responsible. But Hitler converted this already famous "stab-in-the-back" theory into a part of a vast conspiracy: "Jewish" slackers, war profiteers, humanitarians, and Bolshevik trade union leaders, Hitler claimed, worked at the behest of the Western liberal powers, and deliberately humbled the proud Nordic warriors who could not otherwise have been defeated. Those who doubted this were called traitors and confronted with the evidence—had not Woodrow Wilson himself insisted that the mighty German Empire be replaced by a Republic, a Republic ruled by the very creatures who had betrayed Germany, the "November criminals of the Weimar shame"? And did not these traitors, in turn, accept a treaty which tore Germany apart and emasculated her armies? Undoubtedly, few of the more worldly-wise conservatives swallowed Hitler's conspiracy theory whole, but they did find it useful and that is the point. For far more was at stake than simply the reputation of the German military. The prestige and power of an authoritarian social system was in the balance, a system which had justified its autocratic ways to the masses by an impressive series of military victories which had, in fact, created modern Germany.

Furthermore, the German military and its conservative supporters would not surrender their ambition to dominate the East. Again, *Mein Kampf* was useful. Hitler had seen the Slavic masses, as he thought, literally taking over the German Hapsburg Empire in Vienna and doing so in the name of liberal and democratic self-determination. When he saw this encouraged by the largely Jewish-controlled Viennese press with its French cultural orientation, his rigid, lower-middle class mentality detected traces of a leftist international conspiracy to rob Nordic Germany of the just fruits of her power. Hitler, like many militarists, was a crude and brutal Social-Darwinist. "The first rule of life," he once remarked, "is defend yourself!" Peace is the frightened cry of the weak and the unfit. Again and again in *Mein Kampf* he repeated his one complaint about previous German conservative leaders: They had failed to follow the iron logic of the international racial struggle for survival. As he said more than once, "The German people owe everything to the German Army." In the end, it was Hitler who, with a vast array of non-Nazi support established, however briefly, the German Empire in the East, and launched vast extermination programs to alter the racial balance so as to favor the survival of Nordic humanity.

Hitler's conspiracy theory, in short, recast traditional conservative ideas so as to make them attractive to the lower-middle classes and to his own immediate following—a motley crew of lower civil servants, bank clerks, small businessmen, retired war horses, *lumpen-bourgeoisie*, and Central European café ideologists. Furthermore, the conspiracy theory justified, in the name of ultrapatriotism, the most vicious deeds against those whose crime was that of rejecting conservative interests and values. Liberalism and socialism were equated with treason (this is still done by the radical right everywhere) and patriotic loyalty was enlisted in the conservative cause. Thus ran the lock-step equations of *Mein Kampf:* Liberals who called for national self-determination were really out to contaminate Nordic blood with Slavic and to destroy the German Empire. Democrats were really agents of foreign powers who hoped to weaken Germany by undermining her venerable system of the natural selection of a ruling elite. Jewish businessmen, really agents of international Jewish finance, were starving German workers in order to cause social unrest and drive good Nordic businessmen to the wall. Trade union leaders and Socialists were agents of international "Jewish" bolshevism, whose aim was to tear apart the Fatherland through class struggle and revolution. Modern culture (e.g., cubism was a creation of French and Marxist Jews according to Hitler in *Mein Kampf*) was meant to destroy the ancient and solid sense of Germanic morality and introduce the degenerate spirit of moral relativism and sick hyperindividualism. Much of fascist "irrationalism" can be better understood when its social function of uniting old and new conservatives is understood. In the closing pages of *Mein Kampf* Hitler put it clearly: The Nazis are the only political group which knows how to find a mass following for conservative racial nationalism and can rescue its values from the onslaught of liberalism and leftism.

Racists are those who identify mental traits with physical characteristics. The vast array of pseudoscientific racial theories at the turn of the century were eagerly accepted, and often created, by the radical right. Here was a convenient way of explaining social and cultural differences without acknowledging that they are socially conditioned and may be ameliorated by progressive social legislation. For Mussolini's followers, especially after the conquest of Ethiopia, the African was genetically incapable of all but a slave's role, and hence could be ruled as a slave. Hitler's S.S. applied the same theory to Slavic humanity, if with more terrible force. For the white Southerner in the United States, the Negro is inferior by nature, and hence no one can be held responsible for his oppressed condition. The Jews of Europe, however, had wealth, power, and social position, and therefore had to be directly attacked and destroyed. Central and Eastern European fascists held Jews genetically responsible for the "degenerate" and "traitorous" values of liberalism and socialism, and genetically incapable of being reformed or of reforming themselves. If the Jew is by nature evil, his destruction cannot be a crime. Thus an Eichmann can remain, as he reportedly was, a good family man and, after business hours, a solid representative of bourgeois virtue. The conservatives of Central and Eastern Europe had the enemy conveniently located for them by the radical right—in the bloodstream of Jews and Slavs.

The radical right is not always anti-Semitic, as the Italian example shows. But it is normally and perhaps necessarily racist. Fascists cannot recognize the social and historical reasons why conservative values are threatened by change in rapidly modernizing societies—to do so would mean to surrender to the left. Thus, fascists must find absolute villains and conspirators who are not merely stubborn, and hence might be persuaded to accept conservative values, but who are genetically incapable of changing their character and opinions. Depending on the nature and source of the threat to conservative values, the radical right selects this or that group as the object of its racial hatred. As Goering and other fascists put it: "We decide who is Jewish." Hitler exploited the resulting tension of self-doubt and self-inspection—Aryan is as Aryan does. Hitler believed in the genetic determination of mental traits. And, although he admitted that there was no pure Aryan race, he did believe that Nordics were still relatively uncontaminated by Jewish, Slavic, or other inferior blood, and was eager to use force to maintain this relative "purity."

In *Mein Kampf* the details of the alleged international Jewish conspiracy were made explicit. By nature, we read, Jews are sterile, greedy, destructive, and without higher loyalties. As parasites, they are unable to create a science, culture, or nation of their own, and must suck the life-substance from host Aryan cultures. Nations which have allowed this to occur under the influence of carefully contrived "Jewish" theories of liberal toleration, have lost their vitality and fallen victim to the plague—as in France, England, and the United States. Bolshevik Russia itself, in the opinion of Hitler, was clearly in Jewish hands, and yet, because of its latent and fanatic power, the greatest single threat to Nordic humanity. Certainly, *Mein Kampf* is far from being a direct translation of conservative ideas, but that is hardly the point. Traditional conservatives were vulnerable to its lower-middle class vulgarity and radicalism because they were desperate and threatened, or so they feared, by the apparently irreversible trend toward liberalism and radicalism in Central and Southern Europe after World War I.

As G. L. Mosse has shown in his brilliant study, *The Crisis of German Ideology*,[3] the ideas Hitler combined in his conspiracy theory were not unfamiliar to the German and Eastern European public. A generation before Hitler, Pan-Germanic ideas, i.e., autocratic, racial, and bellicose nationalism, were basic attitudes found in significant amounts among all groups with the exception of organized labor and liberal and left intellectuals. The press and popular magazines of Germany and Central Europe had fed a steady diet of racial nationalism to the public since the last quarter of the nineteenth century, and anti-Semitic stereotypes were nothing if not commonplace in German mass culture. In 1918, a viciously anti-Semitic novel, *The Sin Against Blood*, was a runaway best seller. German popular culture abounded in images of sleek Semitic financiers seducing blond and presumably innocent Nordic virgins. The leading German literary circle at the end of the nineteenth century presented the ideas of the radical right in feudal guise, complete with Nordic warrior-knights, the mystic worship of the sacred blood of the elite, and a firm belief that all which was truly Germanic was medieval and "organic." There were hundreds of racial institutes and

[3] G. L. Mosse, *The Crisis of German Ideology: Intellectual Origins of the Third Reich*, The Universal Library, 1964.

racially oriented health-faddist clubs, as well as worshippers of allegedly ancient mystic and Nordic cults of clean-living savages, their vital fluids cleansed, fed on organic foods, and united with the holy Teutonic soil in the collectivist spirit of the racial *Bund.* Hitler himself, of course, was a vegetarian and a humorless food faddist. Himmler had close connections with various mystic Nordic and anti-Semitic cults, as did General Ludendorff. This was all part of the radical right's obsession with the "disease" and "moral decay" of modern urban liberalism. When taken seriously, such images suggest not only food faddism to protect oneself, but also radical surgery to protect society.

Moreover, elementary and high school teachers were, from the 1870s on, overwhelmingly anti-Semitic, antiliberal, and antisocialist, and they trained the modern generation of German leaders accordingly. Sophisticated as well as popular studies of German history were racial, ultraconservative, and imperialistic—e.g., the work of the most famous German historian, Treitschke, who composed ultrapatriotic poetry, wrote ultraconservative history, and hurled diatribes against the Jews for allegedly destroying solid Germanic peasant virtues. By World War I, the dueling fraternities of Central Europe were racist, nationalist, and radical right in politics, and these fraternities contained Germany's potential leaders. Nazi student youth believed, correctly enough, that they were simply acting in the spirit of their traditionally conservative fathers. After the 1880s, the largest white-collar unions for commercial employees were completely given over to the ideas of the radical right. When one takes this in conjunction with the previously mentioned upper class rightists, it is impossible to disagree with G. L. Mosse—Hitler found old and new conservatives alike ready for him in the millions by 1932.

There are those who say that fascist ideology is

basically a product of modern irrationalism, and hence has few ties with traditional conservatism. To demonstrate this they most often refer to the powerful influence of Georges Sorel on the ideology of the radical right in the twentieth century. That influence is not to be denied, though it was largely confined to fascism in Latin countries. Like many fascists, including Mussolini himself, Sorel ranged from left revolutionary to right revolutionary in his political views, though typically—and again like Mussolini—he made no stops at any of the intermediate reformist or democratic positions. (This seems typical of Leftists who become Rightists.) Young fascist intellectuals found much that mirrored their own spirit in Sorel's works. Sorel used the various elitist theories popular during the early years of the century to express his contempt for bourgeois democracy and its presumed love of ease and political compromise, and he accused liberals and democratic socialists alike of being motivated by voracious material appetites and the hunt for well-paying jobs.

Social struggle alone, Sorel insisted, will purge mankind of this degenerate barbarism of sold-out parliamentarians, softheaded democrats, and humanitarian cowards. Thus Sorel exalted the sectarian violence of the idealistic and conspiratorial revolutionary *Bund*, sacrificing its private interests in pursuit of a social myth through an apocalyptic transformation. The fascist movement, in the eyes of its more idealistic followers, was led by an heroic, dedicated, and disciplined elite ready to use any force needed to drive out the soft, comfort-seeking, and eternally compromising rulers of decadent Europe. Neither Sorel nor his followers expressed much explicit interest in realizing any particular myth beyond that of the forceful rule of a revolutionary elite—the function of the myth was to inspire. This "irrationalism" led Sorel at one point to admire Lenin and to call for proletarian violence against decadent capitalists. Nevertheless, like his fascist followers, Sorel ended up on the radical right. In France he worked closely with that assortment of militarists, ultraconservatives, Royalists, and ultranationalists who sought to end the threat of liberalism and democratic socialism by force and terror.

If we forget for a moment the irrationalism of a social movement which claims to have no specific goals—Mussolini's boast—and look instead at the social function of fascist ideology we will, I believe, cease to think it either evidence for the demonic will to power of modern man, or radically different from traditional conservative values. Traditional conservatism, though not its lower-middle class radical variant, is neither terroristic nor totalitarian. When Sorel and other fascists spoke of the superiority of will, myth, and violence over the mere drift of mundane historical forces, they were not really demonstrating their unique and nonrational approach to politics. They were justifying the institutionalization of terror and the dynamic sweep of totalitarian controls, terror and controls which they knew must be imposed if conservative values and interests were to be preserved. For as I have said, fascism came to power in precisely those societies where traditional ruling elites were desperate in the face of spontaneous social changes which favored liberalism and radicalism. To defend conservatism in such societies, the radical right had to forswear political compromise and political democracy, and do so with violence and totalitarianism, otherwise the game was lost. Meanwhile, they had to justify the whole in the name of the higher idealism of the myth of the corporate state. That is the rationale behind the Fascist revolt against reason. This we will see clearly as we turn now to Italy and discuss the first successful seizure of power by the radical right in Europe.

THE SEIZURE OF POWER: ITALY

I am a revolutionary and
a reactionary.
—MUSSOLINI, 1919

In October of 1922, Mussolini and his Fascists took power in Rome. This was the first major political victory of the radical right. The history and social conditions of Italy provide some insights into why this should have occurred, and help us answer the crucial question: What makes a society vulnerable to the radical right?

The radical right seems to flourish best where there is a dialectical polarity between the forces of conservatism and those of modernism. The Italian South resembled nothing so much as an underdeveloped agrarian and semifeudal social system, with a vast, land-hungry, and miserable peasantry oppressed by municipal authorities and police, who were both acting as agents of landowners and gentry. Peasant fatalism and illiteracy, combined with a highly restricted suffrage and a lack of political organization, allowed the northern politicians to rule the South as though it were a feudal fief. From the turn of the century on, however, radical and Socialist leaders turned increasingly to the organization of the Italian peasantry in both North and South. This caused more and more landowners to look to right-wing terrorism to protect their interests. Such terrorists were not mere criminals devoid of political consciousness, but conscious, albeit inarticulate, defenders of the rights of property and the prerogatives of aristocracy.

The decades around the turn of the century also saw the industrialization of central and northern Italy, which created another and different kind of threat from the left. An increasingly strong Socialist party, based upon the highly conscious proletariat of Italy's industrial areas, grew dramatically in electoral strength. Like their famous German counterparts, the Italian Socialists, although nominally Marxist and revolutionary, were in fact revisionists more or less committed to parliamentary democracy. Among them, however, there were a significant number of revolutionary syndicalists, mainly from the South, often strong enough to challenge the moderate Socialist leadership. Perhaps in part due to the rhetoric of this revolutionary minority, the ruling classes were able to keep the Socialist party proscribed and outlawed until 1904. But in the years following, the establishment witnessed an alarming and increasing mass vote for socialism. In 1912, Italy gained universal suffrage, and in that same year, the revolutionary left within the Socialist party won control from the moderates. This meant, or so it seemed, that democracy in Italy would result in the eclipse of the various conservative coalitions which had ruled since unification, and the rise of the masses to a share in power. To those who are inclined to underestimate such fears, it is perhaps appropriate to recall that even such a liberal as Macaulay once begged the House of Commons to refuse the Chartist petition for universal suffrage and a secret ballot because of his fear of the masses.

Until World War I, Italian liberalism and the Italian political system resembled the narrow liberalism of the mid-nineteenth century. Only the propertied few enjoyed the vote, and government was conceived primarily as the defender of property. The Italian establishment ruled by clique through a policy of corruption and fraud in the North and by these plus force in the backward South. Hence the typical spirit and practice of Italian prewar political life: "transformism." Italian politicians, from personal motives, easily "transformed" their political allegiance from ministerial to antiministerial coalitions without higher allegiance to political principles or basic social groups. Too much has been made, however, of the alleged vulgar Machiavellianism of Italian political life and character. Without universal suffrage or mass political consciousness, this form of narrow, propertied, "consensus" politics seems unavoidable anywhere. In Central, Eastern, and Southern Europe, including Spain, parliament functioned as a mere clearing house for corrupt deals; and this quite naturally created a powerful tradition of antiparliamentarianism on both the left and the right. Pareto, an aristocrat who left Italy in 1893 disillusioned with Italian political life, was only the latest and most profound of a long line of observers driven to cynicism by the spectacle of parliamentary failure.

Restricted liberalism and semifeudal conditions in Italy created a strong class antagonism among the exploited groups who were just coming to political consciousness. The result was a modern Italian history fraught with class struggle. For example, throughout the Italian South and the Islands, large and medium landowners combined with local government to prevent vast numbers of agricultural workers from uniting in order to better their lot. Whenever there were land-reform laws, local governments (controlled by landowners) ignored the laws or modified them to favor their patrons. This, together with regressive taxation policies, led in 1893, for example, to extensive and violent uprisings among Sicilian agricultural laborers. Acting as agents for the absentee landlords and their extortionate stewards, the police (and in Sicily the Mafia) ruthlessly suppressed the revolts. In 1898, bread riots in the South, combined with an insurrection in Milan, led to the outright rule of military reaction under General Luigi Pelloux, and the flight, imprisonment, or court-martial and extreme punishment of many Socialist leaders. In September of 1904, the first general strike Europe ever experienced took place in Italy. Led by the brilliant and fiery Labriola, and coming as a climax to peasant attacks on municipal authorities, a general strike was called for by the Milanese Chamber of Labor to counter the brutal repression of the government. For five days in September, Italy seemed at the mercy of the revolutionary syndicalists. The church itself was frightened enough to remove its old ban on the political activities of the faithful, and the fears of the landowners and middle class can only be imagined. Similarly, in 1914 there occurred the famous *Red Week*, when a former Bakuninite anarchist, Errico Malatesta, led a wave of protest and violence which started as a demonstration against the government's use of military force against the left. Prior to World War I, Socialists, radicals, and republicans joined forces in Parliament to protect constitutional government against the militaristic and authoritarian radical right. After World War I, however, the polarization of Italian society was such as to cause a more intense crisis, and this led to a search for a more permanent and extreme saviour for embattled conservatives.

Italian fascism never attained the demonic thrust and

violence of German national socialism. This was due in part to the magnificent humanistic civilization of the Italian past, and the marvelously humane instincts of the Italian people themselves. Otherwise, however, there are basic, if only general, similarities between the rise of the radical right in both nations. As in Germany after Bismarck, so too in Italy after Cavour; landowners, industrialists, and militarists ruled through a monarch. In the last quarter of the nineteenth century, they were not threatened by mass democracy and the effective social radicalism active in more liberalized nations. However, universal suffrage in 1912, rising political consciousness, effective organization among the masses, and a general level of rising expectations after 1918 threatened the very basis of conservative interests. Just as in the Germany of Weimar, but less explosively, propertied oligarchic interests in postwar Italy had to reckon with democratic and radical strivings. The lack of liberalization of the older aristocracies and new business classes in the nineteenth century was indicated by the fact that Italian and German landed and upper-middle class business interests, unlike the French and English, had combined as allies against threats from below. The conservative establishments of both nations had, within living memory, created national unity. This both intensified nationalist sentiment and gave it a conservative thrust.

Nevertheless, by the opening of the twentieth century, the gradual liberalization of Italy seemed certain. The authoritarian and conservative imperialism of Crispi had been replaced by Giolitti's cautious foreign policy and his interest in modest domestic reform. Socialism gathered strength with every year; and the demand for universal suffrage, thought likely to open the gates to social reform, was in the air. Since both socialism and universal suffrage were feared by conservatives, nothing was more natural than an increase of radical right sentiments at the same time. Supported by the army, heavy industry, and the sons of the old conservatives, Enrico Corradini initiated a radical-right nationalist movement which gathered together the anti-Giolittian conservatives in order to stiffen the establishment's resistance to liberalism and socialism. Modeling itself on the *Action Française* royalist movement in France, the new nationalists paid homage to the memory of Crispi's conservative authoritarianism and militant imperialism. Corradini's literary followers spoke of the need for the firm rule of an heroic elite; the superiority of the concept of the organic state over liberalism and individualism; and the need to stop pampering the masses, the democrats, and the Socialists. Referring to his doctrine as a "national socialism," Corradini called for internal unity, economic and military power, the exaltation of the martial virtues, and the establishment of an Italian Empire in the Balkans and Africa—in short, a program similar to that which Mussolini would propose after the war.

World War I intensified both sides of this dialectical process of polarization. For Europe in general, but for Italy and Germany in particular, World War I was a disastrous blow to what had been the steady progress of democratic liberalism. The mud, filth, and senseless slaughter of the war seemed to demonstrate the utter bankruptcy of Western bourgeois civilization, and engendered revolutionary attitudes on both left and right. Moderately conservative circles now succumbed to right radicalism and loudly demanded the punishment of those "traitors" and "pacifists" who would not support aggressive imperialism as they had not supported the defense of the Fatherland during the war. Conservative nationalists hoped to have Italy replace Austria/Hungary as the rulers of a Balkan and Slavic Empire. During the war, many on the left, unfortunately for their postwar effectiveness, allowed themselves to be associated with neutralism, or, like the Socialists, foolishly took the worst possible stand by officially proclaiming that they would neither help nor hinder the war effort. In general, however, liberal left opinion stood for a quick end to hostilities, a negotiated and just settlement, and freedom for the subject peoples of Austria.

In the immediate postwar chaos, the right enjoyed most of the advantages. The right held that Italy had won the war and lost the peace—the so-called "mutilated victory." Dissatisfied with gaining only Trentino and Trieste, they insisted upon Allied recognition of Italian claims to a Dalmatian Empire. Like the first Nazis, they called traitor all who supported the peace settlements. Just as the forerunners of the Nazis battled in the East to keep the Slavs at bay after World War I, shock-troop *arditi* joined the poet of the radical right, D'Annunzio, in a dress rehearsal of Fascism—the illegal and spectacular conquest and rule of Fiume in 1919. Like Hitler, Mussolini made his postwar debut for the radical right by leading terrorist gangs of ex-soldiers and sons of the bourgeoisie in breaking up meetings of liberals and Socialists, men who were trying vainly to demonstrate that only a just peace and the renunciation of imperialism could help insure that another generation would not be destroyed in the trenches.

Nationalist frustration during the postwar period in Italy attracted the sort who became the backbone of the radical right in Europe in general—ex-officers, bourgeois students, sons of landowners and industrialists, and the lower-middle class. Inflation and the collapse of the *lira* had their usual deadly effect on fixed incomes, salaries, and pensions, with the result that the radical right gained additional support from desperate defenders of small property and fixed salaries—office workers, teachers, civil servants, small businessmen, and independent professional people. Returning from the trenches, young ex-officers found their sacrifices scorned and their patriotism derided by the left. Unemployed, they faced the great status threat of immersion into the proletariat. They were joined by patriotic bourgeois youth, too young for the war itself. The relatively high percentage of lower-middle class in Italy made their search for an outlet for social frustration all the more favorable to the radical right. Moreover, Lenin's success in Russia had persuaded many on the left to employ a violent rhetoric which caused more than a few to look to the radical right for protection from revolution. After all, conservatives are the traditional defenders of social stability in the West and a genuine fear of chaos aids their cause.

One of the first and most powerful groups to support the radical right was the landlord class, which was threatened by the spread of radical ideas among the agrarian proletariat of Italy. Some 55 percent of Italians lived by agriculture. The vast majority held marginal plots of land or were simply wage-earners. Pulled from the narrow limits of their isolated villages to form the backbone of the Italian armies in World War I, the peasants gained from the experience a new awareness of their political and social debilities and their possibilities for the future. Indeed, to assure themselves of the loyalty of their peasant-soldiers, the conservative government of Italy felt compelled to issue written promises of postwar land reform in the very trenches themselves. After the war, in the summer of 1919, large groups of peasants, often with red flags flying, occupied idle wastelands belonging to absentee landlords. This could not be readily dismissed as simply the work of the revolutionary left. The new Catholic Popular party, formed by the priest Don Luigi Sturzo, led Catholic peasants on such expeditions for land, even though his Catholic party, like all such parties, contained powerful conservative interests. Both Socialist and Catholic peasantry fought landlord oppression with arson, boycott, and violence in the struggle for better wages and working conditions. To the landlord with his semifeudal attitudes, any concession to the peasantry was simply a concession to bolshevism—often enough they referred to even the Catholic peasants as "white Bolsheviks." In any event, it is of the essence of a feudal order that masters do not negotiate terms with their subjects. Even more threatening than sporadic violence was the spread among the Italian peasantry of cooperative societies and self-help unions, which reflected a heightened sense of the need to institutionalize long-term means of meeting peasant grievances. There could be no greater threat to arbitrary landlord rule. The big landlords of Italy had always met such acts with violence. When the government of Italy went so far as to sanction some few land seizures under limited conditions, many important landlords looked for an extra-parliamentary force to organize and institutionalize their counterterror. Thus they came to support the radical right and eventually Mussolini. Traditional despotism and casual violence, it seemed, could no longer do the job.

The postwar period also saw what eventually became a vast threat from the industrial centers of Italy. By 1920, socialism had made truly explosive gains. Something like a quarter of all municipal governments had fallen into the hands of Socialists. Trade unions, workers' cooperatives, and working-class institutions of all descriptions were growing at a phenomenal rate, with a drastic rise in strikes and occasional factory seizures by the workers. As the result of a famous industrial dispute in the Romeo factories of Milan in August, 1920, for example, workers responded to an employer's lockout by occupying the factories. Far more threateningly, they continued production under trade union leadership. This was no longer simply a maneuver for wages and conditions, this was a daring proposal for a new social order. In the end, the workers capitulated. Their leaders were not ready to carry out the revolutionary implications of their occupation. Giolitti, sensing that they could not succeed, did not use force to push them into revolution. The radical right, however, wanted total victory, and it attacked Giolitti for his refusal to use the army and police against the workers. The rights of property had to be defended without limits. Memberships and money poured into the rapidly emerging leadership of the radical right—Mussolini and his Fascists.

The right cannot be satisfied with small gains, for it fears the general drift of society itself. In this, the November, 1919 parliamentary elections were crucial. They indicated that if mass democracy were to continue, Italy would soon be in the hands of the leftist social reformers. Out of 508 seats, Socialists gained 156; Catholic Popolari 101; and what might be classified as dissident Socialists, welfare democrats, and liberals favoring social reform got 148. Frightened conservatives, as in Germany later, now saw that democracy would mean an era of land reform; tax reform; welfare legislation; confiscation of war profits; antimilitarism; and, most dangerous of all, a government responsive to the needs of the masses. Everywhere the "Bolshevik menace" showed itself. There is really little point in asking if there really was a Bolshevik threat. To conservatives, the very proposal of these measures constituted such a threat.

Paradoxically, the Fascists suffered a smashing defeat in the elections of 1919. Mussolini himself was defeated in Milan by the Socialist Turati, 180,000 votes to 4,064. Mussolini had formed his Fascist party in March of 1919, in a hall in Milan donated, sensibly enough, by a local merchants' association. He had already been expelled from a leading position in the Socialist party's revolutionary wing; and his early programs, though basically conservative, contained many attacks against the old reactionary classes as well as against "bolshevism." Such two-pronged attacks are, as we have said, typical of radical-right party programs before the rise to power. Although the right needed Mussolini's services, they would not support anyone who attacked them as well as the left. Hence Mussolini's total defeat in November, 1919. During the next year and a half, Mussolini demonstrated how well he had learned his lesson. He made his famous transition from a passionate, Sorelian, left-wing defender of revolutionary syndicalism, to a passionate, Sorelian defender of the property rights of the establishment, and embraced the conservatives' stern determination to oppose the shibboleths of western liberalism and democratic socialism.

In judging social movements one must not overestimate, as is almost always done, the personality of the "leader." There were many would-be Hitlers and Mussolinis on the radical right—those who succeeded in reaching the top leadership were those who knew when and what to sacrifice or compromise on the road to power, like all successful politicians. Both Hitler and Mussolini purged their own left early in the game. This was not mere cynicism, but politics, i.e., a deliberate adjustment to the political realities of the societies in which they hoped to succeed. Neither utter cynics nor complete fanatics can lead social movements to success. Mussolini disguised his repudiation of revolutionary left radicalism behind a pragmatic philosophy of action which was, in fact, a true reflection of his violent personality and passionate urge to reach the top. Hitler learned from his abortive *Putsch* in 1923 what Mussolini had learned in the elections of 1919: The radical right cannot come to power without the support of the army, the police, the landowners, and the big industrialists—and it cannot get such support as long as it appears even mildly leftist. As Mussolini said when appealing for conservative support after his repudiation of his leftist past, Italy needs a dictatorship, a dictatorship for

> . . . the nation, that is to say the better part of the nation, that which does not go to the left, toward demagogic nullity . . . but goes to the right, towards order, hierarchy, discipline, and has been asking for a true government for three years.

In 1920 and 1921, Mussolini threw his energies into a campaign of intimidation and terror against unions; workers; liberals; leftists; Socialists; and, after 1921, Communists. Led by him, the Fascists destroyed headquarters, institutions, and offices of the left; Chambers of Labor; workers' clubs; cooperative stores; and producers' associations; as well as Socialist and radical printing establishments and newspaper offices. In Tuscany and the Po Valley, landowners used the radical right, increasingly fascist led, against laborers and tenant farmers. Mussolini found supporters among ex-soldiers, young sons of the middle and propertied classes, students, and unemployed workers. As a defender of the "national cause" and its leaders, he attracted the old nationalist groups, such as those who had backed D'Annunzio's storm troopers when they seized Fiume. As in Germany later, local patriotic groups such as the Association for Greater Italy and the Association for Dalmatia merged with the Fascists who also attracted residues of Mussolini's ex-comrades, the revolutionary syndicalists.

The conservatives, of course, had used local and sporadic violence long before Mussolini. But the threat from the left was felt to be such after 1919 that conservatives began to look to the radical right for the institutionalization and organization of a permanent counterrevolutionary force. The primary targets were the institutions of the left, and especially the many municipal governments which Socialists had previously captured through electoral successes. Squads of Blackshirts terrorized and ousted Socialist mayors and local authorities even as they attacked the network of workers' and peasants' institutions. The government stood aside, and the police and army either looked the other way or gave active support. The police and army were strongly right wing. They are, after all, the official defenders of property and the nation, and as such they tend to support the right in all Western nations. Always interested in fighting internal "subversion," the Italian army encouraged its younger officers to aid the Fascists. Throughout Europe, for that matter, fascist movements had influential army and police connections. Meanwhile, the forces of order sensed victory and rallied to the radical right. Even Giolitti's wisdom deserted him. He stood aside, it is said, in the hope that the right extremists would destroy the left. They did, but as in Germany later, they had further aims than merely playing lackey to the reaction.

The Blackshirts, like the pre-Nazi Free Corps of Germany, also carried out a policy of forced repression of internal national minorities, in accordance with their demands for a new Roman Empire in the Mediterranean. Solvene and Croat minorities were violently terrorized and "Italianized." In areas such as Julian Venetia where such minorities abounded, Fascists served as the terrorist wing of the local and previously established ultraconservative patriotic groups. Here, in fact, Fascist Italianization came close to being an official policy of the government even before the march on Rome. To conservatives, the radical right seemed to be carrying out a war of liberation against Slavs,

Communists, and traitors. Where entrenched worker and peasant groups were involved, the struggle reached the dimensions of a civil and guerrilla war.

Mussolini's defense of the conservative establishment against the threat from the left soon bore fruit. The Fascists won 35 seats in the parliamentary elections of May, 1921. They had won none in 1919. Though suffering some losses, the Socialists remained the single largest party. (Had this not occurred, it is doubtful that Italian conservatives would have allowed Mussolini to seize power—they would not have needed him.) Meanwhile, in speech after speech, Mussolini repudiated the vestiges of his Socialist past, and vowed his allegiance to the principles of economic liberalism and the defense of private property. Forswearing earlier Fascist republicanism and anticatholicism, Mussolini spoke in favor of those institutions favored by traditional conservatives in Italy. As for Italy's economic problems, increasingly Mussolini insisted that military force and imperialist expansion would transform Italy into a wealthy world power without peer. Throughout the summer of 1922, private negotiations assured Mussolini that, should he attempt a *coup,* he would have the benevolent neutralism or active support of the propertied; the police; and, above all, the army. The Blackshirts seized some villages in the spring and summer of 1922, and the only significant resistance came from the left. But a general strike called by trade union leadership failed under Fascist counterattack. Negotiations for a normal Fascist entry into the Italian cabinet were broken off when Mussolini, prompted by a few of his more radical followers, realized that there need be no compromise. To his followers in Naples, Mussolini declared: "Either they will give us the government or we shall seize it by descending on Rome." On October 27, 1922, the famous march on Rome occurred, but Mussolini did not seize Rome or Italy. It was given to him. The army and the police openly cooperated with the Blackshirts. At the last moment the King, prompted by his Minister Facta, threatened to declare martial law. His military and civilian advisors told him not to stand in the way of fascism. It is altogether typical that Mussolini arrived in Rome not at the head of a storming band of revolutionaries, but by courtesy of the Italian Railways via sleeping car. Fascism had gained power in Europe. Throughout Italy, conservatives applauded. North of the Alps a more-than-apt pupil found his hero and his model.

THE SEIZURE OF POWER: GERMANY

If the Nazis did not exist, we should have to invent them.
—General Kurt von Schleicher . . . just before January, 1933

It was no victory, for there was no opposition.
—Oswald Spengler . . . just after January, 1933

Germany was, if anything, even more vulnerable to the radical right than Italy. The same dialectical polarities of left and right which brought Mussolini to power worked with even more tension and force to aid Hitler during the Weimar Republic. At the beginning of the twentieth century, Germany was an industrial power without peer; yet she was ruled by a powerful coalition of preindustrial conservative elites who accepted, more or less grudgingly, the partnership of important industrialists and financiers. At the same time, the sweep of German industrialization had generated a threat from the left without parallel in Europe—a massive trade union movement led by the most prestigious Socialist party in the world.

Germany entered World War I with a political system created, in its essentials, by Bismarck in 1871. It combined universal suffrage and apparent parliamentary rule with the actual rule of the Prussian landowning military elite and their allies. Since the Enlightenment, and with increasing force after 1789, this class had resisted all encroachments of what it defined as the alien, un-German, "French and Jewish" principles of liberalism, democracy, radicalism and socialism. Furthermore, as the most valuable, disciplined, and devoted civil service and military class of Europe—a true aristocracy, unlike the played-out parasites of Versailles or the commercialized snobs of London—this remnant of eighteenth-century autocracy had kept itself safe above the drowning tides of liberalism in nineteenth-century Europe. Neither the defeat of Prussia by Napoleon, nor the defeat of Germany by the allies in 1918, could convince this proud class that Germany might benefit from the utilitarian and democratic principles of English shopkeepers and French *petit-bourgeois*.

Bismarck's mighty and fateful achievement was this: The greatest son of the *Junkers* united Germany by means of the power of the greatest Prussian institution—the army. Called to power in 1862 to defeat the liberals' bid for control of the budget in Parliament, he stayed to end their opposition to traditional conservative rule by his victories over Austria in 1866 and France in 1870—victories which catered to the popular, ardent, and obviously justified desire for a united Germany. Bismarck was certainly no Hitler, but this was the political combination that Hitler was to find useful later—military success abroad as a counterweight to the demand for liberal domestic reforms. It is true that Bismarck had to include the great industrialists and financiers of the Ruhr in his conservative coalition; but whatever liberalism may have meant to them, they were willing to accept in its stead the tariffs, subsidies, and amazing economic growth of Wilhelmine Germany. After Bismarck, German nationalism could only be conservative nationalism, and most Germans accepted the Prussian landowning aristocracy and military leaders as the truly "national" German class.

By constitutional arrangement, there was no ministerial responsibility in the *Reichstag*—Bismarck depended for his political position on his Emperor alone after 1871. Furthermore, neither Bismarck nor the Prussian landowning military aristocracy in whose interests he ruled would concede the masses a right to a voice in governmental affairs; and they would not even have allowed such a thing as a Socialist party to exist, had they had their way. They assumed that, as representatives of the truly "national" classes, they had the right to rule without controls from below. It was Bismarck, not Hitler, who first outlawed the Social Democratic party. Bismarck even seriously contemplated a *coup d'état* when the Kaiser seemed about to legalize the Socialist party and otherwise move Germany in liberal directions. Furthermore, to prevent middle class votes from moving to liberals or the left, Bismarck and his conservatives cooperated, off and on, with the radical right, and countenanced anti-Semitism when the occasion suited them. This loose alliance of old and new conservatives was most pronounced during depression years when (as in 1873) such anti-Semites as Wilhelm Marr and later Pastor Stoecker—extremely high in court circles—promoted a radical right ideology of great popularity among the lower classes. To this ideology even a Hitler could add little new of consequence. Bismarck and his conservatives were not Nazis or Fascists, but that is not the point. The danger lay in their use of the radical right to ward off the left when threatened.

Here lies the significance of the steady growth of the Social Democratic party of Germany around the turn of the century. By 1910, the Socialists had the largest single party in the *Reichstag*, with 110 seats. Officially Marxist and revolutionary, the Social Democratic party, once it was no longer outlawed, became reformist and democratic. Thus it became the representative of democratic radicalism and welfare-statism rather than revolutionary Marxism. This made little difference to the ruling elite, however, and none whatsoever to the radical right, to whom liberalism and democratic socialism, even if taken at face value, were but the prelude to bolshevism. When, in 1919, the Social Democrats became the leaders of the Weimar Republic, the fear and hate of old and new conservatives alike built to a crescendo of paranoiac magnitude.

World War I radicalized existing social tensions in Germany and cleared the path for extremism. Germany's conservative landed, military, and business classes had hoped for an increase of German territory and wealth through the conquest of France, Belgium, and Russia, and a German empire in the East. At first, the revolutionary left (and, as the war ground on, the democratic left) called for a negotiated peace without annexations. The Treaty of Brest-Litovsk, which ended the war with Russia, demonstrated what sort of victors the German ruling elite would make: vast territories, 56 million inhabitants, and 80 percent of Russia's coal and iron production were seized. Hitler began his career as a public speaker attacking the Versailles Treaty and defending that of Brest-Litovsk. He was to end his career in vain pursuit of this vision of a vast empire in the East.

More than an eastern empire was involved, however,

for the loss of World War I also seriously undermined the prestige of Germany's former rulers. Germans themselves increasingly failed to see the sense of Prussian rule if unaccompanied by Prussian victories. Any prestige that was to be gained from the pointless massacre of 10 million of the best young males of a generation was gained by the liberal nations of the West. Autocracy by agreement, Bismarck's creation, dissolved. The Weimar Republic was parliamentary and democratic, with ultimate responsibility placed in the mass electorate and the Socialists in power. In the confusion and chaos of the immediate postwar period, one thing was perfectly clear: Should Weimar endure, *Junker* landowners, militarists, and their industrialist allies would, at last, have to come to terms with democratic liberalism.

Liberalism and Socialism posed an immense threat to the political and economic interests of the old elite in very specific ways. Military leaders could not permanently accept a government which acquiesced in Germany's disarmament and the reduction of the army to 100,000 men. *Junker* landowners, leaders in both army and civil service, were quite aware that sooner or later a democratically elected parliament with full budgetary powers would end the subsidies and special economic advantages given previously to the rulers of the eastern provinces of Germany. Land reform itself might come to the aristocratic estates of the East, and with it an end to the profitable exploitation of agrarian wage earners. The industrialists of Germany, faced with Socialist rule, were haunted by the fear of high wages, increased union activity, progressive tax policies, and perhaps ultimately nationalization itself. The Bolshevik victory in Russia was but a year or so old, and the European upper bourgeoisie, like the radical right, could hardly be expected to make subtle distinctions between democratic socialism and what came to be called communism after 1921. Autocratic and ultranationalistic German conservatism could not permanently coexist with the Weimar Republic. This was the alien, un-German liberal revolution the establishment had always feared. From the start, the conservatives carried on an underground war against the Weimar Republic. In this struggle, they were forced to employ the radical right as their shock troops, just as in Italy.

Nothing could have been more disastrous for German liberalism than to have its fate tied to the enforcement of the unfair and humiliating Treaty of Versailles. But it was not to be avoided. Victors cannot be expected to give fair terms after such wars. Consequently, the German radical right and conservatives in general were able to attack as treasonous every concession the government made to the Allies, even though these same conservatives were never willing to renew the conflict in the West (the cost of violating the Treaty). Thus liberalism, already regarded as alien and un-German, could be made to seem part of a gigantic plot to destroy Germany by alienating its territory, draining its wealth by reparations, stripping away its colonies, and forbidding it from continuing Bismarck's great work of uniting all Germans in the Reich. To the German masses, unfortunately, the Weimar Republic seemed to be just what Hitler (and Ludendorff and Hindenburg as well, for that matter) said it was—the defender of Germany's shame. Throughout the 1920s, conservatives and ultraconservatives argued with great effectiveness that Weimar liberalism was the cause of social ills: social ills which in reality were brought about by the war itself or by Germany's failure to carry out progressive social reform at home. The unsophisticated were easily convinced. Traditional conservatives needed no convincing.

As in Italy and Eastern Europe, political life in the immediate postwar period in Germany saw the spectacular but transient rise of the revolutionary left—a Soviet Republic declared in Munich in 1919, and, of course, the famous Spartacist revolt in Berlin itself. As occurred in Hungary after Béla Kun's short-lived Soviet, the right quickly gained the upper hand, for of course it had superior forces in traditional societies. Noske himself, the leader of the Social Democrats, was forced to put down his own revolutionary left with the German High Command and units of the Free Corps, the very precursors of Naziism. It is difficult to see what else he could do. Like their Italian equivalent, but on a much larger scale, the Free Corps were soldiers still in uniform, fighting for the national cause. In Germany, they carried on an illegal underground war against Poles, Latvians, and other Eastern peoples in the hope of retaining German dominance and stemming the advance of bolshevism. All over Germany, moreover, with the support of traditional conservatives, hundreds of armed ultrapatriotic societies sprang up (not radically different from our contemporary "Minutemen" of California) to prevent the forthcoming "Communist" takeover. Unlike the Minutemen, of course, these groups could point to actual communist successes. The Free Corps units in the East attempted exactly the same imperialist drive that Hitler was actually to carry out later. Led by aristocrats and high regular army officers, they fought to protect the big landowners (Baltic barons, Mecklenburg nobility, etc.) from reformist radicalism among their peasants. And they fought for a German Empire in the East. For the first time since 1848, German peasants in the East were actively trying to improve their lot. Already in the early 1920s, traditional conservatives turned for support to the radical right, as they were to do en masse in 1933. Nor were the Free Corps limited in their political ambitions. They did not have to wait for *Mein Kampf* to understand that Germany's mission was ultimately to overthrow bolshevism in Russia itself.

Mussolini won in 1922. It is surprising that the German radical right was not successful as well during the general European right reaction of the early 1920s. Perhaps the main reason was the conservatives' fear of Allied interference in Germany. Too much stress has been laid on Hitler's personal role in any event. There were many small groups resembling the Nazis in the early 1920s. But the conservatives, from Hindenburg down, were not yet ready to take on the Western Allies in battle—as might have been necessary had they then moved against the Versailles Treaty. Thus the first coup by the radical right, the famous Kapp *Putsch* of 1919, ended in a voluntary retreat in the face of a general strike of workers. Kapp, significantly enough, was both one of the founders of an important conservative party and a high official of the East Prussian Provincial administration. He led the famous Erhardt Brigade of the Free Corps in overthrowing the Republic and had himself named Chancellor. The leaders of the German army, in their typical a-political fashion, had refused to defend the Republic. As one of their leaders put it, "The army does not fire on the army." The army leadership regarded republicanism as immoral (as did many millions of upper and middle class Germans) and thus justified the army's treason.

During the years 1919, 1920, and 1921, the German middle classes tended to vote for "liberal" parties, if by liberal one understands unqualified defense of the rights of private property. By 1924, however, their votes had largely reverted to the nationalist-conservative parties. One major cause of this was the terrible inflation of 1921–1923. By 1923, a German currency did not really exist. Though the holders of unmortgaged real property—factories and land—prepared for prosperous years, great segments of the middle class faced ruin. Inflation had destroyed the small man's business, farm, savings, or pension, and left him with a dwindling income. The radical right could not but benefit as the good, thrifty, hard-working, and stolid lower-middle class German found his values denied by events, and his existence imperiled by both capitalist big business and radical big unionism. At the height of the inflation (January, 1923), France invaded the Ruhr to force reparations payments and rashly encouraged Rhinelanders to separate from Germany and form an independent state. The right found it easy to gain converts from those desperate middle class groups who thought the lesson plain: Germany's inflation was not due, as the left maintained, to regressive tax policies and postponed war costs, but was in fact part of an Allied plot to ruin Germany. France unknowingly played Hitler's game. Only a powerful Germany can become prosperous, he was to say again and again, otherwise it will always be victimized by international "Jewish" and Western high finance. The German army continued to recruit its "Black" or illegal units; the right in general made heroes out of men who had the courage, however short-sighted, to fight the French (Leo Schlageter, for example, bravely martyred). The liberals and the left resolved on passive resistance short of war. It was the only real choice, but as usual, the right oversimplified the issue and made political capital from this "treason." During the early 1920s, hundreds of German liberals, radicals, and Socialists were assassinated, usually with impunity, by the terrorists of the radical right—the German judiciary was overwhelmingly committed to the antiliberal traditions of the German past. In law journals by articles, and on the bench through acquittals or ridiculously light sentences, the judges of Germany demonstrated their historical commitment to the German right.

On May 1, 1923, Hitler carried out maneuvers for 5000 of his followers in Bavaria, their arms mainly supplied by the regular army. After the fall of the short-lived Bavarian Soviet Republic, the radical right counterreaction dominated Bavaria. This is why Naziism found its home there. Dozens of armed irregular units existed, ready to save Germany from "Jewish and Marxist" Berlin. On November 23, Hitler and Ludendorff—the very symbols of the coming alliance of old and new conservatives—marched together in Hitler's famous *Putsch.* (It was not the only *Putsch* attempt by the radical right that fall, though it had captured, in Ludendorff, the most prestigious representative of the old regime next to Hindenburg.) The police halted them with a deadly barrage. Ludendorff was set free, however, and Hitler was let off lightly. The right, by definition, could not really commit treason in Germany in the eyes of the conservative judiciary. However hot-headed, they were patriots fighting for good German principles.

But Hitler learned more than this bit of common knowledge. Hitler discovered what Mussolini had learned four years before. Only with the support of police and army could the radical right gain power. As he wrote *Mein Kampf* in the following months, he composed not merely the ideological testament of the German right extremists, he also communicated this political lesson. He repeated his theme more than once: Mass support for conservative ideas and a legal "revolution" are the ways to power for racial nationalism.

The Stresemann period, roughly 1924 to 1929, illustrated what it would take to weaken the appeal of the radical right, i.e., continuing prosperity and (modest) foreign successes. Unfortunately, much of the prosperity of 1924–1928 was based on extensive foreign loans, and had no solid basis in mass purchasing power or progressive tax policies. Still, under Stresemann the inflation ended, profits and even wages recovered, the occupation stopped, international treaties guaranteeing European borders and renouncing war were signed (Kellogg-Briand, Locarno), and reparations were scaled down. Yet even Stresemann, a moderate conservative nationalist, was embittered by his own middle class business following. They refused to accept reasonable tax reform, and even joined the ultraright in calling Stresemann a traitor for his refusal to promote authoritarian militarism at home and military adventurism abroad. As for the great German Conservative party (DNVP) representing Germany's social elite and some 10 million voters, it spoke as follows:

> With all our hearts we hate the present form of the German state because it denies us the hope of freeing our enslaved Fatherland, of cleansing the German people of the war-guilt lie, and of gaining necessary *Lebensraum* in the East.

Depression and inflation, as is well known, increased the appeal of the radical right. But too much has been made of the effect of these postwar economic crises. Increasingly, even under Stresemann, the sons of Germany's old conservatives were turning to the radical right, not because they suffered from inflation, depression, or joblessness, but because they feared that a "westerner" like Stresemann might bring Germans to rest easy with the Weimar Republic. What is certain, however, is this: The National Socialists became, during the early 1930s, the conservatives' last and best hope of staving off liberalism. Obviously, the Depression was crucial, because mass discontent gave Hitler's party the millions of votes needed to defend the remnants of the Bismarck system. As is well known, the Nazi vote increased dramatically with the deepening depression of 1930–1933.

In 1928 the Nazis received 2.6 percent of the total vote, and in 1932, 35 percent. Increasing foreclosures, recalled mortgages, as well as unemployment, brought votes to the Nazis from the older middle class parties and new voters who wanted more than the simple, sterile, and negative defense of property which was all these parties offered. Voting for Hitler was not normally, however, a matter of conversion from modern liberalism to conservatism, but of moving from conservatism to ultraradical conservatism. Many have held that traditional conservatives did not switch in vast numbers to the Nazis, but remained more or less true to their older conservative parties. Many *did* switch, however, but something more subtle and not often taken into account must be noted: Traditional conservatives, such as those in the powerful Conservative party did not need to switch. Their parties offered a right-wing authoritarian nationalism which, if more staid, was not basically different from Hitler's public program of the early 1930s.

The new voters gained by the Nazis tended to be self-employed small businessmen, small farmers, small-towners, lesser civil servants, white collar workers, independent lower rank professional people, domestic servants, artisans, shopkeepers, and the like—generally protestant. For these groups, the Weimar Republic (excluding the religious factor) seemed to offer a dismal future; moreover, they had suffered terribly through both the inflation and the depression. Traditional conservative parties have never had much sympathy with the plight of the lower-middle class. As for the left, to its cost it has always ignored and scorned the legitimate social grievances of such groups even when, like orthodox Marxists, it does not go so far as to predict with glee their demise through proletarianization. Small businessmen saw trade unions pricing labor beyond their capacity to pay. The artisan found his skills less and less useful in an age of technology worsened by depression. The small farmer, usually indebted, was faced with being driven into the landless proletariat by foreclosure and declining prices. All were threatened by a loss of status, all the more crucial in a class characterized by self-inflated pride and enjoying only minimal distinctions between itself and the next class lower down in the social scale. White-collar workers and lower civil servants, for example, were made desperate by the thought of being cut off from the ruling elite with which they had traditionally identified.

Hitler and the radical right in general offered a social policy favoring such groups. The Nazis glorified rural Germany and the "Nordic virtues" of the small peasant and his family farm as against their "un-German" (often Jewish) mortgage holders. They promised the peasant that degenerate urbanites would have no place in the future *Reich* of warriors and peasants. Artisans and small businessmen were promised easy credit and protective laws against the superior competitive power of big business. Civil servants and white-collar workers were urged to look forward to higher salaries and pensions, and a society built to reflect their traditionally conservative values. Social psychologists have often noted that groups with little sophistication and much insecurity often adopt extremist political programs. That is true, but one ought not forget that even the traditional conservatives of Germany (whether landowners, army officers, or industrialists), who were sophisticated enough to find Hitler and his crew distasteful, felt insecure enough to help him to power. The point cannot be made too often: One does not need to be a fascist to support fascism, any more than one needs to be a Communist to support communism—all depends, in a society in crisis, on one's judgment as to future possibilities and comparative evils. Few of those who supported Hitler could know that, in the end, this meant extermination camps; World War II; and, more likely than not, their own destruction.

The social crisis of the 1930s found the ruling elite of Germany still hoping to halt Weimar liberalism without reaching for their ultimate deterrent, Hitler. The radical right posed a threat to traditional conservative ways as well as a promise of preserving them. This was the significance of the rule first of Bruening and then of von Papen from 1930 through 1932. Through these two representatives of traditional conservatism, it was hoped to establish a presidential dictatorship under Hindenburg and thus return, without the direct rule of the radical right, to the essentials of the Bismarckian system. Article 48 of the Weimar Constitution allowed for emergency rule by Presidential Decree, and Hindenburg in these years became the real source of near dictatorial powers. In effect, as A. J. P. Taylor observed, German democracy had fallen a good two years before Hitler came to power. Using Hindenburg's authority, Bruening was independent of parliamentary majorities.

Bruening, at Hindenburg's direction, continued the old policy of direct economic aid to the great landowners east of the Elbe, a policy that went back as far as Frederick the Great. During the election campaign of 1930, one of Bruening's ministers at a meeting of the Patriotic Eastern League called openly for war in the East as the best way of solving Germany's economic problems and her alleged need for *Lebensraum.* Hitler, meanwhile, rapidly gained both financial and electoral support. In September of 1930, the National Socialists scored a landslide unprecedented in German political history. Nazi parliamentary representation soared from 12 seats to 107. This made them the second largest party. It was clear that the radical right had gained immensely from Bruening's rebuff at the hands of the

Allies when he tried to form a Customs Union with Austria, especially since the Depression itself was popularly thought to have been a result of drastic reparations payments to vengeful enemies. In the situation thus created, the middle groups and parties of German political life foundered.

A further indication of the coming coalition of old and new conservatives occurred when, in 1931, a political alliance (the *Harzburg Front*) was formed between the elite traditionalists of the German Conservative party, the veterans of the *Stahlhelm*, and the Nazis. When it came to social crisis, the right, unlike the left, seemed able to unite. It was almost as if the radical right and radical left stood alone facing each other across a great abyss created by inflation and depression. Thus, in the presidential elections of 1932, Hindenburg received 18 million votes, Hitler 11 million, Thaelmann (Communist) 5 million, and Dusterberg (middle-of-the-road) 2.5 million. That is to say, of approximately 37 million votes, 34 million went either to the radical left or the radical right. Many Social Democrats and Weimar supporters, it is true, voted for Hindenburg as the last defender of the Constitution. This delusion was all that was left to republicans, liberals, and moderate Socialists. What had been true of the Eastern provinces and Bavaria now seemed true of all Germany—as the current saying had it: "A sincere Republican was regarded either as a miracle of nature or a traitor." Sensing victory, the right (both traditional and radical) called for more aid to the landowners of the East, immediate repudiation of Versailles and reparations, an end to trade union "arrogance," the smashing of Socialists and Communists, legal measures restricting the civil rights of Jews, and a drive to bring all Germans into the Reich—including Austria and the Sudetenland. These were not simply Hitler's policies, but policies of conservatives in general, including Hindenburg; the policies that had gained more than three out of four German voters in the presidential elections of 1932.

Bruening himself was dismissed in May, 1932, when he suggested that perhaps the landowners of the Eastern provinces should accept a modest amount of land reform and a resettlement program designed to aid some few of the millions of unemployed. For this, he and General Schleicher, the most important "political" general, and of course conservative, were labeled "agrarian Bolsheviks" by those closest to Hindenburg. With such a definition of bolshevism, the conservatives needed Hitler, especially in view of his mounting votes. For, after all, even if traditional conservatives supported in theory Hitler's drastic and radical right-wing policies, they had neither the dynamism nor the utter brutality such solutions to Germany's problems required.

On January 7, 1932, Hitler spoke to the elite of Germany's industrialists at Düsseldorf. It was his most famous speech. He appealed to them to continue and increase the large sums they were contributing to his mounting campaign expenses for the hectic and frequent elections of the 1930s. He assured the industrialists that rearmament on a vast scale would provide them markets and end unemployment. What he had written in *Mein Kampf* he now stated explicitly: Weapons would solve Germany's economic difficulties, difficulties which were caused by weakness in the face of allied pressure and lack of adequate *Lebensraum*. As to the left, it would be smashed. Most important of all, perhaps, he told them that no matter what they might have heard, national socialism stood for the sacred rights of private property. Only if these rights were honored, he insisted, could Germany gain the economic strength needed for a policy of iron determination abroad.

Still reluctant to choose Hitler—after all an upstart

who had achieved no more than corporal's rank in the war —Hindenburg selected Major von Papen to replace Bruening. A fifth-rate arch reactionary from the Catholic nobility who had married the daughter of a wealthy Saar industrialist, von Papen formed a cabinet of "gentlemen and nobles" to try once more to make Bismarck's neofeudalism function in an age of industrialism and mass democracy. Papen himself was a devotee of the Catholic, medieval, and organic state, as were many of his class. Acting for Hindenburg, he tried to gain support from the Nazis without giving them any significant power. The Nazis were allowed to rule the streets, the ban on their S.A. toughs was lifted, and they and their "fellow travelers" were even allowed to take over the government of Prussia and purge it of liberals and Social Democrats. Even so, Hitler attacked von Papen as a traitor unwilling to use Germany's power to redress her wrongs.

In July of 1932, the Nazis doubled their supporters as nearly 14 million Germans voted for Hitler and gave him 203 seats out of 608. Given Germany's many political parties, this was another unprecedented and smashing victory. But the left (Socialists and Communists) remained as strong as ever. Nothing could be more significant. For it was this which made Hitler necessary to upper and middle class conservatives alike. In one last vain attempt, Hindenburg chose General Schleicher to replace von Papen as Chancellor. But Schleicher fell because he angered the court circle around Hindenburg. Once again policies which anywhere in the West would have been regarded as conservative gained for Schleicher the title of the "Socialist General" from stubborn and short-sighted reactionaries. Finally, at the home of an extremely influential representative of banking and industry, von Papen personally offered Hitler a share of power, if he would agree to a secondary role. But Hitler, like Mussolini before him, sensed that he need not settle for a normal parliamentary role. He held out for the post of Chancellor and was given it.

The conservatives who helped Hitler to power believed, we are often told, that they could manage him and cast him off when the crisis abated. Perhaps this is so, but it is only a small part of the story. The main delusion of traditional conservatives was their refusal to see that their demand for a reversal of history could only be carried out by the ruthless brutality of Hitler and the iron logic of his lower-middle class extremism. Conservatives did not understand that if they were serious in their demand for the rigid defense of their interests and values, they would need Hitler. They would need his totalitarian controls and finally his militant imperialism to make good their claims to rule unmolested by liberals, Socialists, and workers. Hitler did defend the landowners of the Eastern provinces from land reform. He did guarantee markets for industry through rearmament. He did stop militant trade unionism. And he did maintain authoritarian militarism. But those who willingly accepted this much did not foresee that all this could not be done without grave risk of Germany's destruction and their own.

Hitler's lower-middle class supporters were the most deceived of all. To them, Hitler offered ultranationalism pure and simple. All of his arguments removed the blame for Germany's ills from the shoulders of the ruling classes, and placed it on the Western Allies, international Jewry, bolshevism, and the "treason" of the Weimar Republic. The inflation was blamed on Versailles and the French occupation. "International Jewish capitalism" was held responsible for the ruin of honest Aryan small businessmen and tradesmen. "International Jewish communism" had weakened the patriotism of the workers and their willingness to perform honest labor to create a powerful Germany. To the price-squeezed and indebted small farmer, Hitler offered subsidies and *Lebensraum* for resettlement in the East. In short, Germany suffered because of an international conspiracy of Jewish Bolsheviks, British gentlemen, decadent Frenchmen, and hypocritical Yankees. Moreover, Hitler continued, the bayonets of the Allies were the only real force that stood between the true German spirit of obedience and discipline, and the corrupt parliament of thieving Jewish radicals, intellectuals, and internationalists in Weimar. Meanwhile, having deprived Germany of her colonies, did not the West continue to exploit half the world and deny Germany her empire in the East?

There was even less in all this for the lower-middle class than there was for traditional conservatives. Only the power of nationalism and the social frustrations of the inter-war years could have impelled the German lower-middle class to accept its own destruction so willingly. Whatever else one concludes, one thing is certain: Hitler won in Germany because he appeared as the champion of both the reactionary militarist, aristocratic, and business establishment, and the nationalistic sentiments and social despair of the bulk of the German middle classes.

THE FAILURE OF FASCISM IN SPAIN, ENGLAND, AND HUNGARY

Failure teaches as much as success, even where social movements are concerned. In different ways, Spain, England, and Hungary illustrate the historical and social conditions which hinder the rise of fascism. But there is nothing exhaustive or even particularly compelling about this selection. France rather than England could be used to illustrate the obstacles facing the radical right in a thoroughly liberalized nation. Rumania, rather than Hungary (or Spain), would shed light on fascism's widespread acceptance but essential failure in what we now call "underdeveloped" nations. England and France both teach us that the disappearance of strong semifeudal groups combined with the more or less thorough liberalization of social classes and institutions makes it unlikely that significant numbers will find revolutionary conservatism overwhelmingly appealing even during times of acute social crisis. From Hungary, Spain, and Rumania, on the contrary, one finds that where modernization has not occurred, older conservative elites may be strong enough to rule without the need of fascist totalitarianism, terror, and imperialism. The rule of a Franco, a Horthy, or a Carol may appear fascist. In reality, however, these regimes are not dynamic and totalitarian but old fashioned and authoritarian, which is possible only because of the weakness of the threat from liberalism and radicalism. As we have noted, the ultraradicals of the right—whether Fascist, Nazi, Arrow Cross, Iron Guard, Falange, or even American Renaissance party—seem to thrive only in societies where heightened social tensions increasingly aggravate a deep-seated polar confrontation between traditional and modern social groups, both of which are relatively powerful. They seem to fail where traditional conservatives and preindustrial conditions overwhelmingly predominate, or where liberal institutions and values have carried the day.

Fascism in Spain

> Down with Intelligence!
> Long Live Death!
>
> Spanish Fascist slogan.

Franco's government is not fascist but authoritarian—i.e., more or less the direct agent, not of revolutionary reactionism, but of landowners, church, industry, and army. In spite of the prevalence of social violence and anarchism in Spain, there never was a truly massive and long-term liberal and radical social threat. Those broad historical movements necessary for such a threat simply by-passed

Spain: the Renaissance; the Reformation; and, more significantly, the Enlightenment and modern industrial capitalism. Consequently, even the Spanish "liberal" middle class of the nineteenth century was largely a landowning class which absorbed feudal values. The social basis for Spanish republicanism was extremely feeble, and consisted mainly of journalists, school teachers, professional people, intellectuals, and a scattering of lower-middle class elements. The bulk of Spaniards could, far more easily than the Germans, regard the liberal principles of 1789 as alien, brought by foreign invaders (under Napoleon) from a nation given over to atheists, Freemasons, liberals, and Jews. Indeed, only in Spain did Napoleon's armies meet disaster after disaster at the hands of peasants who were carrying on guerrilla warfare designed to support feudal and religious values and interests.

Spain was and is characterized by the persistence of preliberal political institutions and social values. Thus, for example, Carlism—a movement dedicated to monarchical and religious absolutism, the return of the Inquisition, and above all the extirpation of liberalism—is still an important political force in Spain. Throughout the nineteenth century and finally under Franco, armed Carlist units fought Spanish republicanism. Its supporters were found among the less-well-off aristocracy and sections of the more prosperous landowning peasantry of the North. Only an underdeveloped European country could have produced such a powerful rural movement upholding king, church, and fatherland. It has been said that the Carlist's only surrender to modernism was their adoption of the machine gun. The Spanish church—an ally of Carlism—had increasingly identified itself in the nineteenth century with the Spanish upper classes in a mutual attempt to uphold the social values of seventeenth-century Spain. The church was a major social force in Spain, owning some one third of Spain's capital wealth and dominating education and culture. In the twentieth century, bishops and priests continued to lead the battle against the liberal and republican attempt to separate church and state. As a Spanish Catholic catechism of 1927 put it:

> Question: What kind of a sin is committed by one who votes for a liberal candidate?
>
> Answer: Generally a mortal sin.

The landowners of Spain, whether titled or middle-class, upheld a feudalism which, it has been observed, was mainly distinguished from that of medieval Spain in that it recognized no obligations toward the peasantry. Spanish landowners ran their local districts and villages with exploitive techniques even more extreme than those of southern Italy, rigging elections, avoiding taxes, pressing wages to the lowest limits, and taking terrible revenge on those who protested. The army provided its notorious Civil Guard, always ready to shoot down strikers and unarmed peasants and to oppose anarchist terror with more extreme counter-terror. What is regarded as corruption in the bureaucratic technocracies of the bourgeois West was for the Spanish upper classes an unselfconscious way of life. The Spanish army, though it had done battle through the nineteenth century with the reactionary Carlists, was clearly identified with the aristocratic and landowning classes; and these classes provided the bulk of the army's officers. Far more than the Prussian army, the army of Spain looked upon itself as the repository of all that was truly national and, in an emergency, the rightful and legitimate ruler of Spain. Again and again in the nineteenth century, the generals ruled by decree as direct agents of Spanish conservatism.

Consequently, and in spite of universal suffrage, Spanish politics in the twentieth century was little more than a series of elections managed from above. Political life in Spain was led by men who represented no political or social principles beyond their immediate interests, men whose main concern was to work out acceptable personal deals with one another.

The long-term and well-organized liberal and radical national forces that made the rule of the Italian and German establishments increasingly unstable did not reach serious proportions in Spain. Yet the prevalence of anarchism and syndicalism among the field and factory workers of modern Spain has led many to assume the opposite. (There was a relatively weak but disciplined Spanish Socialist party—Marxist and revisionist in nature as in Italy and Germany—but anarchism and syndicalism were far more widespread.) Spanish anarchism was not the kind of threat from the left, however, which requires the sweeping dynamic of totalitarian social reorganization. Using sporadic terror and military despotism, the Spanish right found it possible to suppress the movement. Spanish anarchism was openly contemptuous of political organization, bourgeois compromise, and bureaucratic techniques—and hence easy to oppress. Anarchism and syndicalism were the result of political and economic underdevelopment and a corresponding psychology of violent but uncoordinated political action. Their revolutionary supporters were to be found among the following groups in Spain: depressed field workers and landless peasants in the great arid regions, tenant farmers and sharecroppers paying exploitive rents to often absentee aristocratic or upper class landowners, debt-ridden peasants laboring on large estates, and underpaid factory workers (usually part-time or former peasants) employed in small shops.

Where industry or agriculture was more advanced,

and conservatism less reactionary, Spanish radicalism tended to take a more disciplined, organized, and even reformist character. In such areas, social struggles occurred far less often, but offered a more serious threat to the old elite. As it was, however, in much of Spain the road was clear for Bakuninite anarchism. Orthodox Marxism in the nineteenth century had not yet been adjusted by Lenin and Mao to address the grievances of peasants in underdeveloped nations. Revisionist Marxism in northern Europe, France, and Italy assumed the existence of liberal and parliamentary institutions. Spain had no institutions which could offer hope for peaceful and democratic social reform. As for liberalism, it had no chance whatsoever. As an economic doctrine committed to private ownership, nineteenth-century liberalism had been used to justify the robbery-by-purchase of the peasants' national heritage of common and communal lands. The purchasers were largely from the middle and upper classes. As for liberal political doctrines, such was the government's fraudulent control of elections that, time after time, anarchist and syndicalist districts "returned" Catholic and conservative deputies.

Unrepresented, unable to improve their condition, exploited like colonial peoples by their own upper class, offered not the least chance for a political solution to their ills, it is hardly surprising that the Spanish lower classes were receptive to anarchism. How could they fail to reject the institutions which had rejected them? Many were to find, naturally enough, the basis for a vision of a new social order in their primitive villages and communes. Idealistic, visionary —even Saintly—and therefore terrible in their wrath, anarchist leaders upheld a utopia of self-governing communes and rejected as despicable any compromise with their bourgeois and aristocratic enemies. Committed as they were to local autonomy, the anarchists could not plan for the kind of effective concerted action which depends on discipline, compromise, restraint, and bureaucratic organization. The syndicalists' commitment to the revolutionary act of the general strike was, of course, part and parcel of this natural and resolute refusal to attempt to change the existing order within its limits and according to its rules. Hence the characteristic phenomena of the Spanish left—sporadic risings, peasant revolts, isolated terror, uncoordinated strikes (often with no strike funds), and the dream of returning to the village when the class enemy was defeated, with little further thought for political reorganization. The traditional violence and terror of the ruling classes was sufficient to strike down these risings and revolts. Even under Franco, Spanish society has not been totalitarianized and restructured, merely terrorized and repressed.

Nevertheless, a move to the radical right was generated in Spain in 1930. It came with the end of General Primo de Rivera's rule, the swiftly following resignation of King Alfonso XIII in 1931, and the jubilant declaration of a Republic in the streets of Madrid. For the first time, Spanish conservatism felt mortally threatened. Yet appearances were deceptive. Excluding the larger cities, there was no significant republicanism in Spain. The Republic came to power not because of a vast demand for it, but because it seemed the only real alternative to a bankrupt monarchy.

Conservatives, however, were frightened by the very existence of the Republic. When its legislative plans and its electoral support became evident, Spanish fascism began to thrive. By 1932, the founding date of the fascist *Falange Española*; Carlists, monarchists, army leaders, landowners, and the church began to look seriously to the counter-revolutionary forces of the radical right. What else could one expect, for example, from the proud Spanish aristocracy when it read in the beginning of the new draft Constitution: "Spain is a democratic Republic of workers of all classes." Army leaders heard in fury the Republic's plans to cut the army by half, reduce the military budget, retire many officers (especially known counterrevolutionaries), and commit Spain to disarmament and the peaceful negotiation of all international disputes. The upper clergy of the Spanish church faced the separation of church and state it had always feared. This would mean the secularization of education, marriage, and divorce; an end to state subsidies for priests; the exclusion of religious orders from commerce; and the expulsion of the Jesuits. Cardinal Segura, head of the Spanish church, agreed with the Vatican: Such measures would mean triumph for the spirit of not only Luther and Voltaire, but also Marx and Lenin.

The Republic's frontal attack on the most powerful vested interests of Spain culminated in its proposals for land reform by means of the expropriation of large estates. Many of the grandees of Spain would see their latifundia confiscated should this succeed. Idle estates were to be taken over, as, for the first time, a Spanish government thought to tackle the basic problem of Spain in order to help the poorest and most despised of Spaniards, the landless peasant. As it was, the Republican government reduced rural unemployment and doubled agricultural wages in the first two years of its power. Furthermore, the Republicans' first Minister of Finance, the Socialist Prieto, introduced (quite moderate) "New Deal" reforms to ward off the Depression. Amid grumblings about bolshevism, rich Spaniards deposited their money in foreign banks, the House of Morgan cancelled its Spanish loans, and the international business community declared war on Spanish republicanism—especially after the Republicans purchased Soviet oil at prices under those of the international oil combines. In spite of all this, real wages rose between 1931 and 1935. Tragically and foolishly, the anarchist and syndicalist left, furious at Republican police actions against left-wing violence, began to withdraw its electoral support from the Republic, even as traditional conservatives turned to Spanish fascism.

The Falange was founded in 1932 by José Antonio Primo de Rivera, son of the last military dictator of Spain. The Falange called for totalitarian dictatorship *à la* Mussolini, a corporate state, a renewal of Spanish imperialism, respect for private property, rearmament, and the repression of all the "un-Spanish" ideologists of liberalism and socialism. Their racial myth centered around the exaltation of the passionate violence of the Spanish Catholic personality, as contrasted with the supposed shop-keeping and ignoble spirit of Western materialism and liberalism. As one of Rivera's many Spanish fascist predecessors put it: "Spain is and ought to be at war, in the tradition of the Spanish *conquistadores!*" Or, as José Antonio himself put it: "Our purpose is to unite men's wills against the march of revolution."

Traditional conservatives hoped, as usual, that fascism would confine itself to terrorism against the left, and thereby aid their own aristocrats who were busy drilling armed units in Spain, even while Mussolini's officers trained armed Spanish units in Italy. Falange membership reached about 5000 by the end of 1934, and consisted of sons of the upper classes, students, white-collar workers, professional groups, and unemployed workers. Wealthy landowners, Jesuit bankers, and many industrialists, despite vague fears of Fascist "leftism," made financial contributions. Although the elections of 1935 gave the conservatives a majority, the crescendo of street and rural battles mounted and finally reached the dimensions of a civil war. Thousands of innocents were slaughtered especially after the Foreign Legion was called in by the right.

The elections of 1936 led directly to the Spanish Civil War, for the newly formed Popular Front of the left defeated, if barely, the Conservative Front. The Conservative Front was composed of traditionalists; monarchists; Carlists; Falangists; and, most powerful of all, the CEDA—the party led by Gil Robles which represented the large landowners of the South, the army, and sizeable numbers of upper bourgeoisie. The left had won in spite of the plea of the Bishop of Barcelona: "A vote for the conservative candidate is a vote for Christ." Political murders and raids on political and newspaper offices increased. Conservative money and conservative youth moved into the fascist Falange. But José Antonio could not provide Spanish conservatives what Mussolini and Hitler had offered the German and Italian right. The Falange never swept the field with masses of votes, and Spanish liberalism had not progressed to the point where the terrorism of the Falange was so necessary to the right that conservatives were willing to risk taming Fascist social idealism. The Spanish army, in view of the dispersed and disorganized character of the left, felt fully competent to smash it in the traditional manner. In the summer of 1936, Franco put it clearly. To paraphrase: We Generals will prevent the Popular Front from coming to power. We will suspend the Constitution, the Cortes, and universal suffrage. We will suppress those liberals and leftists who receive their inspiration from abroad. In the event even the alien ideology of fascism was not needed. Franco was a traditional Spanish solution to traditional, if intensified, Spanish problems. The outcome of the Spanish Civil War was not the victory of a dynamic, new revolutionary conservatism as in Italy and Germany. It was the direct and unmediated victory of the old feudal classes of Spain joined by the upper-middle landowning and industrialist classes of the reaction.

Curiously enough, the Spanish Civil War itself may very well mark the high point of Falangist influence. The Blueshirts, along with the gilded youth of the upper classes, acted as terrorists for Franco in occupied Spain, yet also used left Fascist ideas to attempt to win over the "red masses." Perhaps because they never came to power, the Spanish fascists were able, unlike the Nazis and Italian Fascists, to maintain some small amount of the social idealism to be found in all fascist party programs. It was one of Franco's Ministers of Labor, a Falangist, who, purged by Franco at the behest of Spanish industrialists when he attempted to improve the lot of the workers, remarked with anger that Spain was afflicted with the last truly Marxist capitalists in Europe.

Franco has used the Falange on occasion to frighten conservatives, but generally he has kept it at arm's length. Although its members were often rewarded with unimportant but well-paid bureaucratic posts, Spanish fascism has had as its main function that of propagandizing for the regime in order to disguise the intellectual poverty of the familiar system of rule-by-generals for church, landowners, army, and capital. Only when an axis victory seemed near in World War II did Franco give way to Falangist demands for stronger influence, and this ended with the war. Franco bathed Spain in blood during and after the Civil War, and he did it with extreme brutality. Since then, Spain has shown no significant signs of liberal ferment. No "New Order" has been created by Franco because, unlike Mussolini, he has not been driven to find the means to control a massive and spontaneous development of liberal and radical social forces. In spite of the charges of the left, Franco is neither a Mussolini nor a Hitler but, as he has been aptly called, the "uncrowned Carlist King" who presides over a static and authoritarian conservative coalition.

Fascism in England

"HURRAH FOR THE BLACKSHIRTS!"

The headline, *Daily Mail*, January 8, 1934.

In Spain, liberalism was too weak to force traditional conservatives to support their own radical right. In England, the institutions and values of liberalism had transformed society so thoroughly that even during the troubled 1930s relatively few conservatives seriously contemplated a drastic move to the radical right. Unlike their continental counterparts, the English aristocracy was liberalized in thought and political function and could hardly turn violently against Parliament, the institution which had been so intimately associated with their own power since the seventeenth century. Although never convinced of the total validity of classical liberalism, the English aristocracy, again unlike the semifeudal agrarian aristocracy of Central and Eastern Europe, had made their peace with it. The English aristocracy was in fact characterized by its mixed social character —commercial, industrial, urban, and often urbane. England's favorite conservative, Edmund Burke, was not unlike European conservative ideologists with their nostalgia for the organic medieval society. Yet Burke was, in economic ideas, a follower of classical liberalism and, in social thought, best characterized as a very cautious and pragmatic or conservative liberal. As for English industrialists, they had never absorbed feudal values, and had accepted, if grudgingly, the modern labor movement. They were, in fact, *the* liberal class throughout the nineteenth century. Correspondingly, the British left, because it operated within a liberal society evolving (if slowly) toward democracy and social reform, had been relatively untouched by the revolutionary ideologies of the continent—from Chartism in the 1830s to Fabianism in the 1890s. There were, furthermore, practically no traces of the masses of landless and depressed peasantry so common and so potentially explosive in Southern and Eastern Europe. All this is merely to say that England was the classic liberal-consensus model, and suffered hardly at all from the tensions caused by what has been called the dialectic of the extremes.

From the early 1920s on, however, there had been radical-right extremist groups in England; and during the social crises of the interwar years they were able to gain some support by appealing to certain traditional Tory ideas and fears. Many Tories, in view of the great Liberal party victory of 1906 and the subsequent introduction of social welfare legislation, looked upon modern liberalism as England's mortal enemy. The liberals seemed willing to throw away that great nourisher of Anglo-Saxon values—the Empire—as evidenced by their softness towards the Boers, the Irish Nationalists, and the independence movement in India. There were even those Tories who argued that the honest yeoman values of rural England were being undermined by alien ("Jewish") plutocrats with their rootless cosmopolitanism, cunning business instincts, and contempt for traditional British values.

Throughout the nineteenth century, of course, many conservatives had detested Cobdenite liberalism. In their view, the pernicious doctrine of economic individualism had caused the deliberate sacrifice of English collective national interests to the selfish private interests of liberal industrialists. The Corn Laws, for example, had protected both the price of grain and the rural gentry from foreign competition. This in turn, conservatives agreed, made England militarily independent from foreign agricultural supplies, and assured the survival of a stolid, tough, Anglo-Saxon yeomanry. By repealing the Corn Laws in 1846, the Cobdenite liberals had ruined England's traditional rural life, and forced her military to depend on the (allegedly) rootless, nervous, and unreliable stock of the city slums for the defense of the Empire. This sort of traditional conservatism was accompanied by the more sophisticated conservative ideas of many brilliant intellectuals, especially those who made up the Belloc-Chesterton circle. They called for a return to the principles of the organic guild system, a defense of the small businessman against big capitalism and big unionism, and a society based on widespread small holdings—Belloc's "distributionism." Liberal social development in England had, of course, made such ideas even more utopian than on the continent. In any event, as we shall see, where fascism came to power, these forms of radical conservatism were shunted aside in favor of economic policies favoring heavy industry and big business.

During the 1930s in England, such traditional conservatism became radicalized through fear of the seemingly imminent triumph of the Labor party and socialism. Indeed, there existed a significant amount of what Sir Stafford Cripps once characterized as "country-gentlemen's fascism." After the shock of the imposing Labor party victory of 1924, many frightened Tories found it difficult to distinguish between a Ramsay MacDonald and a Lenin. An increase in welfare state legislation, a huge unemployment rate, and left-wing activities brought fascistic groups support from many conservatives—notably landed proprietors, minor industrialists, a few Anglican clergy, and the usual assortment of retired officers from the armed services. When Ramsay MacDonald's Labor government recognized the Soviet Union; and when, in addition, the famous and fraudulent forged letter from Zinoviev was uncovered—a letter "revealing" that the British Labor party was preparing a revolution under Russian guidance—thousands of votes were gained for the Conservative party and Fascist memberships increased. Perhaps the most decisive event was the vast general strike of 1926. Half of organized labor quit work to show support for the ill-treated and striking coal miners. Many conservative members of Parliament were ready to use fascistic strikebreakers and shock troops to protect conservative gatherings and break up Socialist meetings. More than a few prominent conservative leaders responded favorably to the Fascist cry for an end to "milk and water" conservatism, and even to Fascist demands that striking union leaders be shot out of hand.

The swift rise and fall of Sir Oswald Mosley and his British Union of Fascists illustrates some familiar aspects of radical right-wing social movements. Like Mussolini, Mosley had been an important left-wing Socialist before moving to the right. Mosley was at one time high enough in the Labor party to be considered a potential Prime Minister. When he first called for a Corporate State it was a call from the left, from Labor's acknowledged expert on unemployment. He was far from being the only one deeply frustrated by the Labor party's surrender to conservative economic policies during the Depression. In the budget of 1931, with MacDonald's approval, the Conservatives sacrificed the workers' welfare in order to combat the Depression. In turn, Mosley sought what he, like his continental predecessors, had called the "third way," i.e., a new political system to replace the allegedly played-out institutions of parliamentary democracy, one that would avoid both reaction and bolshevism. Returning from a visit to Mussolini, Mosley founded the British Union of Fascists. Like all "left" fascists, he soon learned that the nature of his potential support pushed him swiftly to the extreme right. He recruited a large percentage of ex-servicemen; youth from the upper- and lower-middle classes; and unemployed workers from London, Birmingham, Manchester, and Bristol. Increasingly, Mosley's movement adopted violent anti-Semitism, ultranationalism, militant and aggressive imperialism, and street violence against the left. Further to the right stood Arnold Leese and his few hundred followers, men who scorned Mussolini as too liberal and offered, it may be before Hitler, the gas chamber as a "final solution" to the Jewish "problem."

Such mass support as there was for British fascism, however, was mainly confined to east London where the influx of Jewish refugees from Russia during the early twentieth century had threatened the local English small businessmen, shopkeepers, and artisans. Mosley proposed legal restrictions against Jews—including the outlawing of Jewish chain stores—and financial subsidies and legal protection to tradespeople, clerks, salesmen, and civil servants. Similarly, the British Fascists were able to gain relatively heavy financial support from some business and commercial firms, some of the landed gentry, and a number of wealthy and influential conservatives. The depth of the Depression, in the first half of 1934, saw the height of Fascist influence, not only in east London but among some of the most fashionable circles in London. Many London branches were opened, with *Black House* the aptly named headquarters. Party income reached a half million dollars yearly, and the B.U.F. spent more than the Conservative party itself on propaganda. To frightened and frustrated conservatives, Mosley offered an end to trade union disputes; terror against the enemies of Empire, King, and country; and the dictatorship of a revolutionary conservative elite to smash the left. To support his cause, Mosley gained the not inconsiderable influence of the conservative *Daily Mail*, the first mass-circulation daily in England.

But it was hardly possible for either the radical right or for that matter the radical left to have any serious impact on political life in England even during the worst years of the Depression. The lower-middle class was too well off and too liberal to supply Mosley with significant votes—no Fascist ever sat in Parliament. After 1934, unemployment fell off steadily, and even the most reactionary conservatives found it a little hard to panic in the face of a supposed Bolshevik threat. After all, even in 1931 the Conservative party had won a majority of seats in Parliament, and at no time even under Labor did the British government abandon its essentially conservative policies of retrenchment, budget balancing, and protectionism. As elsewhere, finally, military conscription and arms production increasingly brought England close to full production and full employment. The great industrial strikes of the 1920s did not reoccur; and as for the Communists, they managed to win only one seat during the parliamentary elections of 1935.

Conservatives in England remained true to their own grand tradition in the end, as a wave of revulsion against Mosley's street toughs and storm troopers swept through all groups. Furthermore, Mosley's increasingly open identification with Hitler was no help to his cause, though he could hardly avoid it. Few conservatives wanted to prevent Hitler from conquering Russia as it turned out later. But none had much patience with the idea of reshaping English institutions to fit a foreign ideology and a bloody German one at that. By the end of the 1930s, the radical right in England (as in France) shared the dilemma experienced by any ultra-patriotic movement which models itself on the "New Order" of an old foreign rival. It is difficult, if we follow the European experience, to imagine the success of fascism where no vestiges of the feudal past remain among liberal institutions and industrialism (—it is perhaps too hasty to conclude that the radical right has no chance at all). Yet it seems equally true, if we examine the Hungarian example, that the extremists of the radical right are unable to succeed in societies where there are too many vestiges of the feudal past.

Fascism in Hungary

Western scholars are accustomed to view the political process as a struggle between conservatives, liberals, and radicals. Thus they often misunderstand and patronize the political life of Eastern Europe. For the historical traditions and social development of such countries as Hungary and Rumania, for example, led in the interwar years to the rule of traditional conservatives whose chief rivals for power were not liberals, and certainly not leftists, but rather the revolutionary conservatives of the radical right. As Istvan Déak has observed in his excellent article, "Hungary" (in Rogger and Weber's *The European Right*), from 1919 to 1944 there were two "rights" contending for power in Hungary—the traditional and overwhelmingly predominant landowning aristocratic right of the Regent Horthy, and the national socialist right of such men as Gyula Gömbös and Ferenc Szálasi.

Social development in Eastern Europe, with one or two exceptions, had created no massive liberal or radical threat to the rule of traditional semifeudal elites. In Horthy's Hungary, King Carol's Rumania, and Pilsudski's Poland (as in Franco's Spain), preindustrial ruling elites retained enough control of political affairs to allow them to reject fascism as a means of preserving their authority, values, and interests. In such circumstances, the radical right appears as simply a threat to conservative values. In Eastern Europe, consequently, traditional conservatives often used violence to suppress their own radical right, as when Carol of Rumania had the leaders of the fascist Iron Guard, including the murderous Codreanu, shot out of hand. Thus the traditional right on occasion became, if only by unintended consequence, the defender of what few liberal elements did exist in such societies! Similarly, Eastern European fascists could maintain their social idealism with far more consistency than their German or Italian counterparts since they never were forced to betray it for power. For example, the radical right often defended the interests of small-land-holding peasants against great landowners. This, of course, was the basic reason for their conflict with traditional conservatives, and one reason why power was denied them.

Eastern Europe was characterized by a powerful aristocratic landed class, an extensive small-land-holding or landless peasantry, and a relatively small urban middle class, itself dominated by many failed or lesser gentry. Liberalism and radicalism were represented largely by alien elements—German or Jewish. Both the old and the new right were extremely favored by such social circumstances. It was easy, for example, to persuade Hungarians and Rumanians that liberalism, socialism, and even urbanism were alien products of foreign and Semitic values and "blood." Far more than in Germany, the landed aristocracy and gentry could look upon their values, their interests, their style of life, and their power as truly representative of the national and patriotic traditions of the land. Furthermore, Eastern Europe was characterized by a wide mixture of nationalities, a prevalence of minority ethnic groups within each nation (one out of six belonged to a national minority group), long periods of foreign rule, violent mutual national oppression, and a complex of historic claims and counterclaims. All of this gave ultranationalistic pride and hate truly overwhelming influence. Extreme militaristic and imperialistic attitudes were the norm. Excluding Czechoslovakia, neither the liberalism of the Enlightenment nor the radicalism which accompanied the rise of nineteenth-century industrialism had advanced far enough to pose a potentially mortal threat to such societies. Still, the radical right did come to prominence during the social crises of the 1920s and 1930s, though nowhere did it come to full power except under the direct influence of Hitler's armies.

In Hungary, the imbalance of land distribution in favor of the Magyar aristocracy (and some upper class nonnobles) was unequaled elsewhere in Europe. And more than elsewhere this class stood for national and patriotic traditions. It had led the fight for independence from Hapsburg rule, as well as the often brutal struggle to Magyarize reluctant ethnic minority groups. Below the Magyar aristocracy and gentry stood vast numbers of peasants; at the lowest level were the famed "two million beggars" of landless agrarian proletariat, kept down by conservative legislation, landowner resistance to land reform, and their own fatalism. The practice and spirit of liberalistic enterprise in Hungary was to be found mainly among the "aliens," i.e., Germans; Slovaks; and above all, Jews. The bulwark of urban Hungary, Budapest, was 25 percent Jewish; and this group largely supplied the liberal and radical intellectuals. Jews were heavily overrepresented in liberal callings: banking, finance, commerce, law, medicine, journalism, and culture in general (half of the faculty of the University of Budapest was Jewish). As in Rumania, where Jews were even more overrepresented in the professions, such a social situation was extremely vulnerable to conservative racism. Nor did it help to point out that this overrepresentation was not the result of Jewish racial character, but of Hungary's backwardness and the unwillingness of the Magyar nobility to engage in the much-despised vocations of commerce and industry. The ultimate insult in Hungary was to label any group un-Hungarian. Liberalism was always looked upon by the bulk of the citizenry as un-Hungarian and in some sense treasonous, and so, consequently, were the Jews.

Far more than in Italy or Germany, the results of World War I played into the hands of conservatives and ultraconservatives in Hungary. The Treaty of Trianon literally dismembered historic Hungary, stripping her of no less than two-thirds of her territory and population. This was unavoidable once the war was lost, although it was justified in the name of democratic and national self-determination for the peoples newly freed from Magyar rule. Nothing could have made the ideals of democratic liberalism more unpopular in Hungary, however, for the settlements left three million ethnic Hungarians incorporated into the successor states. The reaction of most Hungarians to this dismemberment was expressed in the famous phrase: "No, no, never!" and could not help but reinforce the ultraconservative cause.

In this atmosphere, Hungary received its first liberal government in October, 1918—that of Count Karolyi. Even in defeat, Hungary's traditional rulers could hardly be expected to accept Karolyi's program: universal suffrage, extensive land reform, and reconciliation with those states recently built at Hungarian expense (Czechoslovakia, Rumania and Yugoslavia). Karolyi soon resigned in favor of a Social Democratic coalition which itself, after a short while, was controlled by the Communist Béla Kun. Thus were Hungarian conservatives confirmed in their suspicion that liberalism was but the prelude to communism, and liberal leaders but potential Kerenskis.

Béla Kun's short reign was a terrible one for the

right. His attempt to nationalize and collectivize the land of his Hungarian Soviet led to violent conflict with both the landed gentry and the peasantry. Béla Kun fled after being defeated by invading Rumanian troops. After this experience, what Hitler with difficulty persuaded some Germans to believe, became easily accepted matters of general opinion among Hungarian conservatives: There is an international Jewish Bolshevik-Allied-Liberal conspiracy (Kun's associates had been largely Jewish), a conspiracy to tear apart historic Hungary and destroy, through bolshevism, her stolid Turanian peasant and feudal culture.

Admiral Horthy, destined to remain as Regent until 1944, swept the counterrevolution to power with anti-Bolshevik committees composed of radical rightists from among army officers; civil servants; aristocrats; and a group which had every reason to hate radicalism, the displaced refugee Hungarians from the truncated historic territories. Retaking "sinful Budapest," Horthy's groups carried out a fearful white terror. Liberals, leftists, and Jews of all political persuasions were slaughtered without mercy. But Horthy never found it necessary to create fascist totalitarianism in Hungary. Such was its underdeveloped character that, like Franco after the Spanish Civil War, Horthy and his magnates and landowners could rule without revolutionary conservatism and its dynamic totalitarian institutions.

The social ferment of the 1920s did bring radical right groups and leaders to prominence and influence, even within the Horthy government itself. There were as many as 200 fascistic groups in Hungary after World War I, including such groups as the *Ragged Guard* (similar to the German *Free Corps*, but here fighting to preserve parts of historic Hungary), the *Hungarian Association for National Defense*, rifle groups, and assorted patriotic clubs. All of these drew heavily on veterans and the lower-middle class for membership, and found significant upper class financial support. These fascistic groups were well represented in the highest governmental circles. But Horthy ultimately had little need of them. With wide-spread approval, he controlled Parliament, selected prime ministers who were responsible to him alone, and defended without serious challenge the traditional privileges of the upper class Magyars. As for the radical right, Horthy was more than suspicious of their support for land reform—this he would never allow. He was even wary of the radical right's purist anti-Semitism, because it was a threat to Hungary's financial dependence on her predominantly Jewish business oligarchy as well as the international business community. Horthy placated the fascists with minor bureaucratic posts, while his judiciary allowed acts of radical-right terrorism against the left and Jews to go relatively unpunished as unavoidable patriotic excesses. The left gave Horthy little trouble. Hungarian socialism existed by governmental sufferance and on condition that it would not attempt to organize the landless agrarian proletariat.

Until the crash of 1929, traditional conservative rule was without serious challenge in Hungary. The Depression and the rise of fascism elsewhere, however, helped bring the radical right to influential governmental position. In September, 1932, the fascist Gyula Gömbös was selected as Prime Minister by Horthy in response to widespread demand. Gömbös never had anything like the power of Mussolini or Hitler, of course, nor did he or anyone else seriously threaten Horthy's power before 1944. The popular demand for some move to the radical right seems to have arisen in large measure as a backlash to the radical demonstrations of workers and peasants which followed hard on the collapse of wheat prices in 1931. The government itself may have unwittingly helped increase support of the radical right by dismissing, as an economy move, sizable numbers of army and civil service personnel—groups always vulnerable to fascist ideology. But in spite of Gömbös' corporate-state ideology, his violent anti-Semitism, and his imperialistic ambitions, he was prevented by Horthy from passing land-reform and anti-Semitic legislation. Gömbös was also prevented from allying with international fascism for what he hoped would be the reconquest of historic Hungary and the eventual destruction of Russian bolshevism. But because, again, there was no real threat from the left, the rule of Gömbös remained little more than an example of the control of fascism by traditional conservatives. After Gömbös' death in 1936 (from natural causes), the radical right continued to prosper and call for out-and-out military dictatorship as well as aid for the depressed lower-middle class and peasantry.

The most important fascist leader in Hungary was Ferenc Szálasi, head of the Arrow Cross Hungarist movement. Szálasi's ideology stressed Fascist idealism, i.e., the superiority of will and instinctive impulse over reason and material limitations. In social terms, this meant the usual *Volkish* nationalism of race, blood, soil, and violence. Nevertheless, Ferenc Szálasi was more of a social idealist than either Mussolini or Hitler, affirming again and again that he did not intend merely to defend the *status quo* of the reactionary classes. In agreement with fascist idealism, Szálasi hoped to create a vast Hungarian "organic" state to rule over the subject nationalities of the Danube basin. His emphasis on militaristic imperialism for the recovery of historic Hungary made him extremely popular among the officer class of the army. He himself had worked in the army's educational branch, always a haven for fascists in Europe.

Szálasi also denounced the "obsolete system of private capital" and its Jewish masters. He criticized Horthy's protection of the Jews, as well as his refusal to punish liberals and Socialists. He hoped to win over the masses; and during his years in Parliament he called for aid to Hungary's peasantry, craft businesses, and marginal tradespeople. Provided with practically unlimited funds by Germany, the Arrow Cross scored a smashing victory in the parliamentary elections of May, 1939, gaining some 750,000 votes out of 2 million. For the first time the government had a real opposition in Parliament, and the world was treated to the spectacle of traditional conservatives repressing by jail sentence and terror their own radical right wing—a repression which continued until the German occupation of 1944 brought fascism to power.

Horthy, without much real choice in the matter, moved into the axis camp with World War II and appointed fascistic prime ministers, such as Imrédy, to supervise Hungary's military commitment to Germany. Those generals who had pushed for an alliance with international fascism were to see half of their armies destroyed in Russia. Perhaps paradoxically, the Horthy right became the last line of defense for liberals and Jews in Hungary, as, egged on by their German masters, the Hungarian Fascists worked for their destruction. When the German occupation finally occurred, Horthy was put into "protective custody." And, with the general approval of many Horthy supporters, Szálasi formed a government staffed with officials from the lower-middle class and aristocracy.

Szálasi's short-lived social program envisioned a renewed and invigorated peasantry, total mobilization, war to the death against the approaching Russians, and the transfer of Hungary's Jews to the Eichmann apparatus.

National Socialist terrorists and Storm Troopers hunted down and murdered army deserters, Jews, liberals, and radicals. By the end of 1944, however, Hungary had received a new government from the triumphant Russians. Thus ended the social conflict between the two "rights" of Hungary.

THE RADICAL RIGHT IN POWER: TOTALITARIANISM AND SOCIAL POLICY IN ITALY AND GERMANY

The greatest tragedy in my life came when I no longer had the strength to repel the embrace of the false Corporativists, who were in reality acting as agents of capitalism. They wished to embrace the Corporative system only in order to destroy it.

—MUSSOLINI, after 1943

We cannot confiscate the property of landlords; we are Fascists, not Socialists.

—MUSSOLINI, before 1943

Once in power, Fascists and Nazis could not (and did not want to) act as mere representatives of what they themselves often contemptuously referred to as the "old reaction." Eventually, the revolutionary right intended to destroy all competing groups, including those which had aided them in their rise to power. In the brief years of rule allotted them, however, neither Mussolini nor the more radical Hitler actually did this. Yet it may be argued that the very dynamism of their reconstruction of society ended by destroying as many conservative groups and values as were saved from liberalism and radicalism by the fascist triumph.

The radical right does not rule with the casual and sporadic terror of old-fashioned autocrats and despots. Fascists and Nazis had to transform social institutions in radical and dramatic ways. As we have noted, only in less-developed countries, where the forces of modernism are weak, can reactionary and conservative coalition governments rule without such a "total" transformation of society—as we have seen with Franco's Spain. Much of the confusion about the "left" or "right" character of fascism comes from our failure to comprehend that the cautious gradualism of traditional conservative theory is incapable of defending conservatism in swiftly modernizing societies. It is then that we are likely to see that peculiarly modern political anomaly, revolutionary conservatism.

To Mussolini goes the credit for inventing the totalitarian state. With the aid of the famous Starace, Mussolini created the essentials of the one-party state during the first six years of his rule. He tried at first to rule in the usual authoritarian style. By 1924, by means of the usual manipulation of electoral laws, street violence, and political alliances, Mussolini had managed to gain 65 percent of the vote in the Chamber of Deputies. In 1924, an important and brave Socialist Deputy, Matteotti, revealed the fraud and terror Fascists had used during the campaign. He was murdered. The press and public outcry stunned Mussolini. This more than anything else drove Mussolini to conclude that he could not rule where modern liberal institutions could still raise a public storm. However weakened and intimidated, a relatively free press, a vocal parliamentary opposition, and a somewhat independent judicial system might still mobilize enough dissident opinion to topple the regime.

At the same time, many of the extremist leaders of provincial fascism protested publicly against Mussolini's "sellout" to middle-class moderation, reactionary landowners, business interests, and military leaders. Fascist extremists wanted to replace the old elite in army and governmental establishment, and silence for good all liberal and left elements. Mussolini could hardly dispense immediately with these older elites, of course, but he could and did move against liberals and radicals. Caught up in the dialectical polarity of left and right social forces which had brought him to power, Mussolini found that he had only two alternatives. He must succumb to the leftward trend of spontaneous social change, or create what we now know as the one-party state. By 1926, the press had been brought under Fascist control, political parties were outlawed, local government regimented, public employment reserved for party members, and the police and bureaucracy purged. By 1928, the Chamber of Deputies was hand picked by the party leadership, and the electorate voted only for approved candidates. A Grand Council of Fascism provided Mussolini with whatever advice he cared to take.

Hitler had Mussolini's example to follow when he took office in January, 1933. He too had started with a Cabinet containing a majority of non-Fascist conservatives. After moving swiftly to assure Krupp, I. G. Farben, and United Steel that his own left need not be taken seriously, Hitler scheduled one last election to demonstrate his power over the masses. Using the *Reichstag* fire to raise the spectre of conspiratorial bolshevism, Hitler gained 17 million votes out of 39 million. The middle parties ceased to exist and the conservative parties suffered heavy losses, but the left held steady at about 12 million votes. The electoral appeal of Hitler plus the continued power of the left persuaded the few remaining conservative holdouts that Hitler must be granted his demand for full dictatorial powers. In the midst of a mounting crescendo of murder and torture, the famous *Enabling Act*, giving Hitler dictatorial powers, was passed. The final act in the seizure of power came in August, 1934, when, within an hour of Hindenburg's death, representatives of the army, industry, and landowners agreed that Hitler might combine the offices of President and Chancellor. The last potential barrier, the German officer corps, saw no need to defend Germany against Hitler. Indeed, they took an oath of "unconditional obedience" not to the Constitution or to Germany, but to Hitler himself.

Hitler, as with Mussolini before, had to purge the remnants of Fascist idealism (both left and right) before he could gain the full support he needed from conservatives. Roehm and the elite leadership of the mighty Storm Troopers (the Nazi private army of some two and a half million men) spoke against Hitler's betrayal of the revolution, and his liking for reactionaries and Prussian generals. Many of the Storm Troopers, unlike Hitler's elite Guard, the S.S., had been recruited from the unemployed workers of the big cities and consequently often favored land reform and prolabor measures. Roehm himself wanted a "permanent revolution" to replace the German army and bureaucracy with Nazis "of the first hour." Von Papen, the Vice-Chancellor, plaintively voiced the lingering fears of the older ruling groups: "Are we going to go through a Marxist revolution after carrying out the anti-Marxist revolution?" At Hitler's direction, Himmler and the firing squads of the S.S.

provided the "final solution" for some 1000 recalcitrant Storm Troopers in June of 1934. The road to totalitarian rule was now clear. As in Italy, bureaucracy and police were purged, local autonomy ended, trade unions and political parties were abolished, and the career of the German one-party state commenced.

Yet even these were conventional restrictive measures, and not enough to stop the spontaneous development of social radicalism in divided societies such as Italy and Germany. Thus, the law itself had to become, as one scholar (William Ebenstein) has put it: "a means for the energetic defense of the state against the dangerous classes." In liberal nations, the law is held to represent abstract or "natural" values, existing ideally beyond the direct manipulation of person, class, or even temporary office holders. Traditional authoritarian governments give lip service to this idea, but violate it by bribe, fraud, and casual violence. Italy and Germany under the rule of the radical right, however, had to reject the very notion of objective law, with its cautious rules of procedure and evidence and its need for clear proof. Judges were purged or intimidated, lawyers were indoctrinated, and both became political agents of the party. The law became the defender of the party's interpretation of the needs of the race and nation. The courts of Hitler and Mussolini made extensive use of such devices as *ex post facto* laws to punish merely potential enemies of the regime, and particular laws and punishments for particular crimes, to ensure that the party had the power to deal efficiently with its intended victims. Inequality before the law became the rule, rights were held to emanate from race or party membership, and police powers were vastly increased at all levels.

The essence of the radical right's view of politics and society is contained in the idea that force rather than reform is the "final solution" to political dissent and social problems. In line with vulgar conservative ideas on crime and punishment, the radical right seeks enemies to punish, not societies to reform. Thus in Fascist and Nazi law, common criminals and political opponents were looked upon as genetically determined, i.e., congenital in Italy, racial in Germany. Using the services of the old conservative Prussian caste judiciary, the Nazis barred Jews from citizenship, the professions, education, government employment, marriage to Nordics, and, finally, from the ownership of property. The same measures were to be applied later to those eastern peoples defined as "subhuman." The law was used not only to punish the crimes of individuals, but to fend off trouble in the future by making suspect groups and classes the object of legal disabilities and punitive legislation before crimes had been committed or hostile political attitudes communicated.

Conservative governments in societies where there is no major thrust toward liberal values can protect themselves from radical ideas by censorship, exile, and prison. In traditional societies undergoing fairly rapid modernization, however, the spontaneous and critical observation of social experience by disaffected groups may well create a political awareness too powerful for such haphazard and sporadic methods. Thus, starting with Italy in the 1920s, totalitarian societies developed the means to control, guide, and give content to the cultural and educational experience of their citizens. Mussolini did much more than merely censor the press. Fascist owners and editors were told what to write, when to write, and how to write it—down to the details. Journalists were simply political agents of the regime. Totalitarian dictatorships must manufacture approval, not merely outlaw disapproval. This assault on the mind would not have been possible without the technology of mass communications. But the radical right does not gain power in technologically backward societies, for in such societies the forces are absent which create a radical left.

Both Fascists and Nazis put schools, textbooks, and teachers under direct party control and detailed supervision. Under the slogan, "Mussolini is always right," Italian children were taught—insofar as such things can be taught—blind obedience, contempt for the humane virtues, and above all an aggressive nationalism glorifying conquest and empire. German youth were taught the necessity of defending Nordic virtues against the ancient Jewish conspiracy for world conquest through racial desecration. Genetic determinism and the "struggle for lifeism" of a brutal social Darwinism were presented as intellectual foundations for a crusade to gain *Lebensraum* (living space) at the expense of the "subhumanity" of the East. Educational institutions had also the task of selecting the new elite. Unlike liberal nations, the leadership could not be allowed to emerge through the haphazard dynamics of unsupervised social mobility. As Starace put it, the revolution must create its own ruling class. The future Nazi elite was trained in Institutes modeled on the famous Prussian academies. In Germany, appropriately enough, the final elite was trained in the "Order Castles" once inhabited by the crusading order of Teutonic Knights. The Teutonic Knights, of course, were experts at spreading Christianity, Germanism, and slaughter among the hapless Slavs in late Medieval times. As is common to the radical right anywhere, counterconspiracy, force, and war were presented as *the* solutions to complex economic, political, and social ills. The method as well as the content of fascist training—one ought not call it education—was totalitarianized. Educational absolutism was the norm, and was enforced by means of the memorized lecture and textbook and the rote drill of classroom recitation. The unique individual judgment of the student, based on his own particular experience, had no place in the system. There could be nothing remotely approaching the liberal free play of tolerant and experimental intellect. The totalitarian mind of the radical right cannot forego the advantages of absolute ideological faith, and hence cannot tolerate the varieties, ambiguities, and give and take of spontaneous dialectic.

The Italian Fascists created a vast network of ideological and paramilitary leisure-time organizations, including the famous *Dopolavaro* (after work) paralleling the Nazi *Strength Through Joy*. Only so could they frustrate the development of spontaneous cultural and leisure activities. Such activities would, if allowed to arise freely, express the independent and hence dangerous varieties of individual, group, or class experience. Normally, each group or subgroup in society can draw upon its own social or work experience as a model from which to judge and accept or reject what it is told or taught by outsiders.

To disarm or gain the allegiance of its citizens, therefore, totalitarian regimes must substitute, where possible, an undifferentiated mass experience and mythology as a counterforce. The mass public theatricalism of totalitarian regimes, for example, was designed to curb any natural attachment to independent judgment. Private and class identity were immersed in the public experience of the parade and the hike; or in the terse, repetitive, and sloganizing speech making and litanies for those fallen in the struggle against the enemy—all accompanied by the massed banners, torches, drums, and trumpets of armed legions. *Volk* mysticism and nationalistic sentiments were used to divert attention from any possible liberalizing elements in one's own experience. Thus Hitler's Labor Service lined up with spades carried on shoulders like rifles, intoning in solemn tones the sacred place names of their Teutonic origins, forgetting (perhaps) their menial tasks and subsistence wages in the racial nationalism of blood and soil. Germany and Italy were dotted with shrines dedicated to the fallen and Institutes identifying by artifact and ideology the radical right with the sacred history of the nation.

Fascist and Nazi architecture itself was an assault on the human perspectives and scale of the individual. The size, mass, and rigid marching columns of their vast marble monuments to war and nation were intended to overawe all that which is merely human, and to inspire the individual to mindless self-sacrifice on these monolithic altars to glory and death. The endless speech making of both regimes was interspersed with the terse fighting slogans and simple images and symbols of militant nationalism. They were intended to drive from the vast shouting audiences whatever remained of critical thought, sensitivity to nuance, and awareness of the true complexities of historical and social change. As one Spanish fascist put it to perfection: "Death to Intelligence." The herd instinct of the tribal *Bund* was to replace the tolerant, urbane, questioning, and essentially free play of the liberal intellect. Typically, the radical right recasts social problems and tasks in the simplistic mythology of war and racial struggle. Thus, to increase the wheat crop, Mussolini's officials spoke of the "battle of wheat"; to decrease unemployment, "the battle of employment." They did not even hesitate to speak in such inhuman terms of that most human activity, the "battle of births." The ideal of the regime, never realized, was to convert citizens into masses and masses into fanatics who would find in terror, armed battle, and foreign conquest, gratifying substitutes for prevailing social and economic frustrations.

Art was used by both regimes to defend the ossified and vulgar conservatism of the radical right from the cultural values of liberalism and radicalism. By law, banal caricatures of monumental realism replaced the experimental, subjective, and varied canvases of postimpressionistic art. The perspectival relativism of cubism and the subjectivism of expressionism (and all art of inner experience), for example, were incompatible with the brutal absolutism and anti-individualism of totalitarianism. Hitler was made especially furious by what he called the "degenerate, Negroid, Jewish, cosmopolitan, anti-Nordic art of mongrelized and Marxist Paris." Official Fascist and Nazi art was warrior-peasant art, expressive of the racial nationalism of *volk*, blood, and soil. Consequently, art in the *Third Reich* was a dreary yet awesome succession of steely-eyed veterans, thick-bodied peasants, and advancing torch and weapon bearers, marching with grim determination, dynamic sweep, and tense muscles into the Nordic future.

Science, and not only the biological sciences, as well as art had to be racial and national. Nordic physicists were asked to reject relativism and the new physics. For the radical right, truth in ideology, art, science, or politics had to be simple, absolute, and final. In physics, as in ethics, Fascists and Nazis could not accept a concept of truth which forsook ultimate absolutes and remained content with hypothetical statements relative to specific conditions; statements varying with observed relationships, and subject to modification by the varieties of new experience. The radical right had—and has—nothing but contempt for the modern pragmatic spirit. The Nazis held modern physics to be the creation of Jews who were racially incapable of finding truth. Thus the work of Einstein and Planck was held to be a part of the general conspiracy against the Nordics, a conspiracy by men who, as liberals unable to conceive of truth, undermined the brilliant achievements of German science by maintaining the swindle that truth did not exist.

Fascist Social Policies

> If the democrats of *Il Mondo* want to know what our program is, tell them it is to break the bones of the democrats of *Il Mondo*.
>
> Mussolini

Once in power, the radical right seems to follow two basic and related policies. It defends conservative interests and values; and it offers militarization and eventually war as the "final" solution to economic and social problems. Thus, of course, liberals and radicals automatically become the opposition, since they tend to support domestic reform and international pacification. In practice, the Fascist corporate state or the Nazi "third way" meant policies of low wages, high profits, autarchy, rearmament, and imperialism. In Italy, wages and working conditions were set by the business community in conjunction with the party bureaucracy. The workers themselves had no real voice in the various labor fronts and Fascist unions organized to control potential trouble. Workbooks and dossiers, plus extreme terror, were used in Germany to weed out possible agitators. Italy, as one foreign conservative said with approval, became the easiest country in which to fight economic crises by pushing down wages and increasing hours. There were Labor Courts in Italy, theoretically (like all Fascist institutions) above class interest; but as Mussolini remarked to the President of the Confederation of Industry, "As long as I am in power, the employers have nothing to fear from the Labor Courts." Even when the complications of the Depression are taken into account, there was a drastic reduction in real wages and per capita consumption of basic foodstuffs in Italy due to the regime's support of the propertied classes.

This held true even during the pre-Depression boom years of the 1920s. As Germany has demonstrated, and not only under Nazi rule, rapid economic growth can result from policies of low wages and high profits. Where the left is strong, however, force and more than force, totalitarianism and institutionalized terror, are necessary to make such policies work. In Germany under Hitler, the gains labor made under Weimar were cancelled; the workers' share of the national income fell; and by every standard, the exploitation of labor increased.

As for rural labor, fascists were brought to power to protect large and medium landowners from agrarian radicalism. Hitler assumed control just in time to prevent a parliamentary investigation into the tax frauds of big eastern landowners, and Mussolini took over in time to set aside proposed laws which would have expropriated some large estates and handed them over to peasants. In order to permanently resolve the land hunger of southern Italy it seemed necessary to carry out a broad redistribution of land. This could not be done, of course, except at the cost of conservative interests. Consequently, the fascists hoped to use the land of conquered subject peoples to end land hunger at home. In general, the living conditions of the peasantry were reduced once their institutions for self-defense had been permanently smashed by fascist terror. As landlords prefer, of course, free peasants tended to become sharecroppers, the "battle of the wheat" was carried on at the expense of the small consumer, and rural landless labor was made to assume great economic burdens under the corporate state. As one of Mussolini's own ministers was led to complain, Italian property owners regarded Fascist social policy as nothing but the enforcement of low wages and high tariffs. Hitler's rural policies were somewhat more determined by the Nazi ideology of the superiority of rural (i.e., Nordic) values. Walter Darré, the responsible Minister, was the author of *The Peasantry as the Life Source of the Nordic Race* (1929) and acted accordingly. Peasant proprietors were protected by supports which, at one point, pushed the prices of German meat and dairy products up to two or three times that of the world market. Those peasants who could claim Nordic blood back to 1800 had their estates entailed by law (and thus made hereditary) and protected from mortgage and debt. Under Hitler, in short, serious attempts were made to realize, first in Germany and later in conquered Europe, the most important reactionary social vision of the nineteenth century —preservation of those remnants of feudalism, the aristocratic landowners and hereditary peasants.

The left has too often ignored or underrated Hitler's greatest domestic reform, the eradication of unemployment. When Hitler came to power in 1933 there were over six million unemployed. By 1937, there were less than one million. Unlike traditional conservative authoritarian leaders, Hitler needed full employment for war production. Indeed, many German workers were absorbed by the heavy rearmament program which had caused an economic boom by 1935. By 1939 the Nazis were spending half again as much on arms as the combined totals of Britain and France. Many workers left the ranks of the unemployed to enter the Labor Service Corps where they worked at subsistence wages on railways and roads. Many unemployed were absorbed by compulsory military service in the rapidly expanding German army. The suppression of the left made possible other policies which reduced the ranks of the unemployed—lower wages, earlier pensions, cuts in living standards, redistribution of work, and higher reinvestment rates. Production was doubled and national income increased, even as the workers' portion declined.

In the drive for increased production, the lower-middle class businessmen, shopkeepers, and artisans who had supported Hitler (and Mussolini) found their interests sacrificed to the superior productive power of big business. In spite of Nazi promises, Hitler could not offend the important business interests that had also supported him. Moreover, he could not repudiate Versailles, end unemployment, and prepare for war with an economy shackled by outmoded guild restrictions. Consequently, Hitler moved swiftly against this "left" Fascism, which was represented by the Feder/Strasser wing of the Nazi party and was embodied in such groups as the *Combat League of Middle Class Tradespeople*. The *League* was dissolved. Hitler banned ideological statements about the Nazi wish to revive the medieval economy of the organic guilds, and legislated in favor of large mergers and combinations. Nothing could be more indicative of the social policy of the radical right than the way in which Hitler, in July, 1934, turned the German economy over to a General Council of the Economy. The council was headed by Krupp von Bohlen and aided by the most important German industrialists and bankers, including Siemens, Thyssen, Schroeder, and the President of the *Reich* Corporation of German Industry.

Mussolini had said in 1923 that his government would "abandon all intervention in the private economy." And indeed, business interests had more or less complete control of currency, taxation, wages, and tariff policies during the first and highly productive years of Italian Fascism. Even during the Depression, when business dependence on bureaucratic party direction and aid increased, the market and production policies, merger agreements, and devices for covering private losses with public funds showed the same tendency to support big business. The social welfare policies of the Fascists—maternity and child benefits, insurance programs, and similar allowances—did not compare in scope with this aid to business, and were related to Mussolini's demand for vast armies for future imperial expansion.

Although both regimes interfered with the economy and directed business policies to a great extent, this should not be taken as evidence for the "mixed" or left-right character of Fascist and Nazi rule. On the contrary, as in Germany, controls were intended to make militarism a means for eventually resolving social and economic problems without recourse to liberal and radical domestic reforms. Hitler used tax relief policies, for example, to push production by heavy industry to the maximum; unorthodox currency policies to the same end were invented by Schacht "the wizard of rearmament"; and companies were forced by controls to reinvest soaring profits in industrial expansion and government loans. By the late 1930s, exports and imports were completely under Nazi control, and enterprises could be established or closed by government fiat. Full production, maximum expansion of the heavy-industry sector, and complete independence (autarchy) from foreign sources of vital supplies were the bases of Hitler's controlled economy. Only thus could Germany free herself from the international "Jewish" market control of liberal capitalism. Only thus could Germany be free for military adventures in Europe.

Fascist states substitute internal terror for otherwise unavoidable liberal and radical reforms which would damage conservative interests. Terror removed or intimidated those who by class, group, or intellectual and religious allegiance could not be expected to share the aims of the revolutionary conservatives. Nazi terror was so extreme as to obscure the use of terror in Italy. Even the worst Italians, it seems, could not create a Dachau or a Buchenwald. When anti-Semitic measures were introduced to Italy in the late 1930s, the Germans who insisted on these programs found Italian bureaucrats placing many obstacles in their way. Nevertheless, Fascist Italy, as one scholar put it, was a "fear-ridden society." There were detention (if not concentration) camps, internal exiles, midnight raids by *Squadristi*, and thousands of cases of torture and murder without due process. What author Ignazio Silone once called the "secret manipulation of fear" was everywhere in evidence. Throughout Italy there existed a vast network of informers in factories, offices, clubs, professional associations, and apartment buildings. The intimidating power of those who control access to place and power even in liberal societies is much underestimated. In Italy and Germany, professional advancement depended in large part on party approval, and even a withdrawn neutralism was highly suspect.

Himmler regarded the majority of the German population as enemies of the regime, including those traditional conservatives who stood in the way of the "permanent revolution" visions of the S.S. leadership. As Hitler once said: "Where we are there is no place for anyone else." The S.S. hoped to make good that claim. In 1933 the first concentration camp was opened. Torture, murder, and pitched battles against the left reached a peak during the first years of the regime, violence especially generated by the lingering fear of a general strike against Hitler. As Goering explained publicly to the police forces of Prussia: "We are not called upon to render justice. Our sole aim is to destroy and exterminate." Himmler already had begun his huge collection of detailed dossiers on enemies, potential enemies, doubtful friends, and political rivals. As in Italy, a gigantic network of informers was built right down to the block level. By state decree, bureaucrats were to inform on their colleagues or be considered themselves enemies of the regime. Professional societies, under Nazi leadership, were required to purge themselves of republicans, liberals, socialists, and Jews—and did so. Thus Goering asserted in 1933:

> Whosoever in the future raises a hand against a representative of the Nazi movement or state must know that he will lose his life without delay. It will suffice to show that he even nursed the intention of committing such an act.

The murder of millions of Jews by the Nazis was not, of course, simply a means of manipulating the fears of Germans or conquered peoples. Nor was it simply a criminal act, or a burst of the demonic irrationality of "modern man." Above all it was not simply an exercise in punishing arbitrarily selected scapegoats. By the murderers themselves, it was regarded as a moral act, a "cleansing" and "purification" of the genetically determined and degenerate racial enemies of Nordic humanity. These deeds were committed by men who were, aside from the actual triggermen, not morally different in any significant way from their fellow Germans. The slaughter of the Jews, that is to say, was a social policy for the alleged improvement of German and European life, and it was an act of German society, not of a few isolated groups of corrupt sadists. The organization of the slaughter had the dimensions of a world war all in itself, and could never have been carried out without the active participation of bureaucrats, businessmen, lawyers, judges, accountants, physicians, foreign-office officials, ordinary politicians, and soldiers, as well as party officials, S.S. men, and the murdering *Einsatzkommandos.*

People from all groups, classes, and professions took part; and there is little evidence of special selection techniques. As one scholar, Raul Hilberg, has said, in those days it was possible to murder thousands by sitting at a desk and signing a shipping order to a concentration camp. Furthermore, when expropriations of Jewish business firms began in the 1930s, thousands of good Nordic businessmen turned a quick profit in blackmail-by-cheap-purchase of Jewish enterprises. Precisely because it was an act of society, few felt the true criminal enormity of the deed. Not only Eichmann, but most of those who participated, excluding the final assassins, could remain solid representatives of the virtues of middle class family life and private honor. Even Himmler could boast, "To have gone through this and yet remained decent, that is what has made us great." The point is not that many Germans were criminals, but that they did not know their acts were crimes.

Both traditional German conservatives and the German middle classes, as we have seen, have a long history of political anti-Semitism. Hitler took these ideas seriously and outbid all competition in the terrible logic of his proposed final solution. His purpose was to cleanse Germany and Europe of *all* diseased groups, and it is crucial to remember that he did not include only Jews in this category. With support throughout German society and not only in Germany, Hitler began to exterminate members of religious sects, dissident intellectuals, "surplus" Slavs, Socialists, Communists, gypsies, political leaders of conquered nations—and even mentally ill Nordics and some categories of the deformed and sick. Death was *the* social policy of the *Third Reich*, death to the enemies of radical right-wing extremism. It was not Hitler or Himmler but an official of the foreign office who told shocked foreigners that "the destruction of the Jews is not a matter of humanity or religion, but of political hygiene." The radical right cannot reform society so as to meet the objections and potential social power of its liberal and radical critics. Indeed, the more sincere ideologists among them believe their critics to be "conscious agents of an international conspiracy bent on world domination" and already extremely successful elsewhere. How cope with critics such as these except with permanent imprisonment or immediate death? Himmler put it exactly when he told his killers: "Do not lose your courage, for future generations will thank you for overcoming your Christian weakness and finishing this good but dreadful work."

FASCISM, WAR, AND IMPERIALISM

There have been states so constituted that conquest becomes a necessity of their being. If they are to continue they must be forever concerned with further extensions of their power.

J. J. ROUSSEAU

We demand land and territory for the nourishment of our people and for settling our surplus population.

NAZI PARTY PROGRAM, 1920

He who has steel has bread.

MUSSOLINI

Let me say at the outset that I am well aware that there are many conservatives and many varieties of conservative thought and practice which shy away from a strong commitment to war and imperialism. For the regimes of Mussolini and Hitler, however, the conquest and permanent exploitation of subject peoples was an unavoidable consequence of their rejection of domestic reform. And even here it may be said that the revolutionary right radically intensified and pushed to extremes those existing and predominant conservative values which did stress the virtues of a warlike culture: authoritarianism, discipline, unity, disdain for dissent, and disregard for the well-being of the masses. Before 1914, Italian landowners, industrialists, and high army officers had subsidized a small but vocal Nationalist party whose program and leadership, in the late 1920s, merged indistinguishably with that of the Fascist party itself. From the beginning of the twentieth century, the Nationalists had insisted upon the suppression by force of all internal enemies of authority and unity—the left. Italy could solve her domestic difficulties only by militarizing the economy and conquering the Balkans and upper Africa to gain power, prestige, and wealth. As Mussolini later put it, the proletarian nation, Italy, had to conquer wealth from the plutocratic international imperialists. Significantly, this was all that remained of Fascist "leftism" once power was attained. Both Italy and Germany, of course, had hoped to complete their unification by gathering in those fellow nationals who still remained outside their respective fatherlands. Neither nation, however, had been as imperialistic before the rise of fascism as, for example, France or England. Excluding Crispi's disastrous attempt to found an African Empire in 1896 at Adowa, Italian leaders (especially Giolitti) had preferred domestic reforms to external adventures. But World War I had stimulated anew the nationalistic radicalism of the right. D'Annunzio's seizure of Fiume in 1919 gave to the radical nationalists a sense of the benefit which they, and Italy, might gain in the pursuit of empire.

As the 1920s progressed, Mussolini militarized the culture and economy of Italy. More and more he spoke of the Balkans and Africa as the place for modern Italy to take up the heritage of the Roman Empire. More and more he encouraged party ideologists to stress Italy's need and right to nourish herself at the expense of foreign lands. Fortunately, Mussolini's Italy had neither the industrial might, the militaristic tradition, nor the disciplined inhumanity which the Germans could put at the disposal of Hitler. The logic of Italy's vulnerability and Germany's power, furthermore, worked to favor a policy Mussolini followed until he invaded Abyssinia—cooperation with France and England, and hostility to German attempts to violate the Versailles Treaty. Increasingly, however, the pressures generated by the Fascist suppression of internal reform, the Depression, and the natural (but not inevitable) international allegiance of the radical right caused Mussolini to ally with Germany in a policy of imperialistic expansion. As one indication of the relationship between domestic reform and imperialism under fascism, we may take Mussolini's much-advertised means of resolving land hunger in Italy. A few war veterans were resettled in the reclaimed land of the Pontine marshes, where landlord interests were not at stake. But nothing significant could be done unless Italy could conquer and resettle the Balkans and Africa, and thus appease land hunger without cost to landowners. Mussolini apparently hoped to postpone a general war until Italy was fully prepared, perhaps in the mid-1940s; but he did not hope to avoid one. As it was, Italy could hardly expect anything but disaster from the alliance—either defeat with Germany, or even worse, victory and the permanent status of a Nazi satellite. Nevertheless, in the 1930s Mussolini spoke of an inevitable war, and insisted that Italy could never become a world power without economic independence from a potential Anglo-French sea blockade. With Hitler, then, Mussolini embarked on a policy of autarchy by subsidizing wheat production and rewarding the search for substitute fuels, metals, nitrates, textiles, and other vital war supplies.

By 1934, Italy was caught in the general economic crisis. The nature of Fascist support ruled out, of course, New Deal or Popular Front reforms. Unemployment rose and production fell. Mussolini publicly despaired of Italy's economic future. It may very well have been that the often-discussed invasion of Abyssinia then became fixed policy. In any event, controls for militarization were drastically extended. State aid to rearmament and related industries climbed abruptly, ever higher rates of taxation (even hitting the wealthy) were imposed, and new controls over the money market directed surpluses and profits into reinvestment. As in Germany, small businesses and craft enterprises were sacrificed to combinations, mergers, and large industries. Internal tensions increased, and even some Fascists were heard to grumble as they foresaw the coming substitute of war for reform. Nevertheless, downward trends in wages stopped. In 1938, there may even have been an increase in real wages, accompanied by a boom in war industries and a decrease in unemployment, evidently caused both by the general economic recovery and the mobilization of labor and soldiers for war in Africa.

Mussolini, who had invented the one-party state, now pioneered in moving toward war and imperialism as social policies for resolving the internal tensions of revolutionary conservatism in power. Thus in Ethiopia, however feebly compared to Hitler's later demonic endeavors, Mussolini tried to create the Fascist new order. It is not so much the bombing and gassing of native soldiers and civilians which is here relevant, nor even the slaughter of thousands of "unpacified" natives after formal hostilities had ceased. Far more indicative of the social role of imperialism under ascism was Mussolini's attempt to form warrior-peasant communities in Africa. These were to be resettlement areas for Italy's surplus population. This surplus itself was in part, of course, stimulated by state aid and subsidies to very large families as a means of forming mass armies to conquer the very "living space" required for the Fascist new order. As a famous slogan put it: "Africa, a land without people; Italy, a people without land." It was not, of course, the surplus population which required imperialism; it was the domestic tensions unleashed by Fascist rule. However incomplete, the African policy was a preview of the coming fate of Eastern Europe and Russia under the rule of the Nordic rather than the Latin master race.

As many have noted, when anti-Semitism came to Italy in 1938, it had little impact. This does not mean, however, that the radical right in Italy was not racist. The Africans and not the Jews or Slavs were, for Italian Fascism, the genetically determined inferior subhumans. Anti-Semitism aside, the function of racism was to justify the subjugation and exploitation of "inferior" peoples—just as it is today among the conservatives of say, South Africa, Rhodesia, South West Africa, or for that matter, the American South. In any event, Mussolini's surrender to the logic of Fascist internal dynamics led, in short order, to the conquest of Ethiopia: the intervention to aid Franco in Spain; and finally, however reluctantly, to Italian participation with Hitler in World War II.

Although the Nazis made imperialistic expansion their major social policy, they did not invent the justifying ideology. From the days of the first French Revolution, conservative and pan-Germanic nationalism was racist as well as imperialist, and maintained the right and even duty of Germany, as noted earlier, to rule over the inferior peoples of the East. These ideas were not little-noted and half-forgotten obscurities. Rather, they had a strong following among the most prestigious intellectual, social, and political groups of nineteenth-century Germany. Among others, one need only mention Arndt and "Father" Jahn, the founders of German nationalism, along with such giants of culture as Richard Wagner and Heinrich von Treitschke. Long before Hitler, the leaders of Germany's most important school of geographical studies called for a resolution of Germany's "living-space" problem—by means of the conquest of the East and its colonization by Nordic peasant syndicates. Kaiser Wilhelm II was, next to Hitler himself, the most prominent fan of Chamberlain's Social-Darwinist racist imperialism. After 1890, there was an outburst of pan-Germanic ideas, from Bernhardi, with his popular and crude call for autarchy and the conquest of the East, to the most refined of German intellectuals—symbolized by Moeller van den Bruck who, though he personally found Hitler distasteful, had himself called for a holy war to resolve Germany's *Lebensraum* difficulties. There are real differences between traditional conservative imperialism and Hitler's radicalism, but they should not be overstressed. Ideas, after all, cannot enter politics and remain pure any more than intellectuals can. By the end of the nineteenth century, there was a flood of pseudoscientific literature calling for expansion by conquest. This was put out by some 50 conservative-supported institutes devoted to attacking liberalism and pacifism and praising the instinctual life of blood, soil, and war against subhumanity.

In his *Origins of World War Two,* A. J. P. Taylor raised an academic storm by treating Hitler's foreign policy as simply a traditional policy of pragmatic power and interest-of-state considerations. Yet it was in fact Taylor himself who, in an earlier book, *The Course of German History,* pointed out that Hitler's foreign policy was new and revolutionary in that it resulted from his regime's need to conquer or collapse. From the days when Hitler composed *Mein Kampf*, the most strongly emphasized of his political ideas remained his call for the destruction and permanent occupation of Eastern Europe and Russia. It seems only fair to quote A. J. P. Taylor on this, if only against himself:

> The alternative to foreign success was achievement at home . . . [which meant] the breaking up of the great estates, the destruction of the hold of the great monopolies, and the diversion of German economic power from foreign conquest to the service of the German people, in short, social revolution. . . . Economically, politically, spiritually, Germany had to keep up a ceaseless process of expansion. Victories on an ever greater scale were its life-blood; and without this increasing flow of victories, not merely the National-Socialist dictatorship, but the entire German order would have collapsed.

Germany's social and economic problems were to be resolved forever by the transformation of Europe east of the Elbe River into something very like a vast concentration camp, supervised by model villages of Nordic peasants ruled by the S.S. elite. Those of the subject peoples who survived the war and the vast extermination programs were to be workhorses for the ruling elite. Thus by war Germany would be freed forever from the threat of international capitalism and international bolshevism; and this without the sacrifice of those interest groups which had supported the Nazi bid for power. In speech, ideological statement, and government directive, Hitler indicated that through the armed might of a renewed Germany, he would put at German disposal the industrial, mineral, agricultural, and human resources of the East. The mineral wealth of Russia alone, Hitler explained to a group of industrialists in 1932, would pay for the German army. To the small-land-owning peasants who had supported the Nazis in such great numbers, Hitler could offer his vast resettlement programs. A Nordic peasant elite would rule over the rich wheat basins and labor sources of the East. To the army, Hitler offered war, conquest, and the permanent rule of a huge empire of subdued Slavs. To German industry, Hitler offered a vast protected market for unlimited expansion. Hitler even hoped to gain the support of German workers through a high wage policy made possible by heavy reliance on slave labor from conquered Europe. In short, Hitler planned to meet the crises of the 1930s with force rather than play the uncertain bourgeois games of international trade and domestic reform.

Far from being an irrational, impractical, or suicidal gesture, then, the invasion of Russia in the summer of 1941 was the essential element of Hitler's foreign policy, precisely because it was the essential element of his domestic policy. From the start, Hitler fairly ached to invade Russia. The war with France and England he regarded as no more than an important side issue. In November, 1937, Hitler told his assembled Chiefs of the Army, Navy, and Air Force, as well as his War Minister and Foreign Minister, that the Nordic values of the Germanic "racial core" could only be preserved if, by conquest, all Germans were brought into the *Reich* and if, furthermore, new territories were conquered to "solve the need for space." Hitler was the very embodiment of the radical right's desire to find a "final solution" to all social problems. This, indeed, was his basic difference with traditional conservatism. Many of those who supported Hitler, as I have said, did not want perpetual party dictatorship, World War II, or the New Order of the East. Hitler, however, rightly saw that most of what they did want could be gained by such means. In politics, one always gets more than one bargains for.

Correspondingly, Hitler's vast arms programs were not intended simply to end unemployment but to make Germany unimaginably wealthy and powerful through war. This, Schacht, Hitler's economic chief, discovered when in 1937 he protested that too much rearmament and autarchy was damaging because it interfered with production of consumer goods and sacrificed German well-being. "You are not really one of us National Socialists," Hitler is said to have remarked when he fired Schacht and replaced him with Goering—who was. Goering put it clearly to Germany's economic elite—it is not any longer a question of producing economically, just of producing. Hitler hardly put it better when he said to a delegation of representatives of heavy industry: "To me, the cost of putting German industry on a war basis is absolutely indifferent and irrelevant."

By the late 1930s the tensions created by a crash program of arms production, a vast extension of spending and public controls, deferred consumption, and the exploitation of labor had done their work. As T. W. Mason has observed in a brilliant article in *Past and Present*:

> The only "solution" open to this regime of the structural tensions and crises produced by dictatorship and rearmament was more dictatorship and more rearmament, then expansion, then war and terror, then plunder and enslavement. The stark, ever-present alternative was collapse and chaos, and so all solutions were temporary, hectic, hand-to-mouth affairs, increasingly barbaric improvisations around a brutal theme. . . . A war for the plunder of manpower and materials lay square in the dreadful logic of German economic development under National-Socialist rule. The sequence of international events was not thereby predetermined, but the range of possibilities was severely circumscribed.

Throughout the 1930s, consequently, Hitler may have pursued apparently "normal" tactics in international diplomacy, and he may have used the "normal" rationale of traditional international bellicosity and discourse, but total war in the East was always the goal. Of course he hoped to neutralize France and England without war in the West if possible, but he did not count on it. Much of the attack scholars have launched against the Western policy of appeasement at Munich loses its force when the dynamics of Nazi foreign policy are understood. Until the destruction of Czechoslovakia, Hitler could easily justify his foreign policy with traditional arguments. No one would seriously suggest, for example, that only Fascists refuse voluntary submission to a treaty denying equality of international status. Most Germans and many foreigners rightly thought that the Versailles Treaty ought to be adjusted in Germany's favor. When Hitler called for rearmament, when he marched into the Rhineland to remilitarize what was, after all, German territory, he was only doing what every self-respecting electorate in an age of nationalism demands of its leaders. Even the German invasion of Austria had much approval in Austria itself because of a long-standing desire to complete German unification. The invasion and occupation of the *Sudetenland* was wrong and aggressive, but even to most non-Nazi Germans, all Germans belonged in the *Reich* and the Czechs had no legitimate claim to rule over the Sudeten Germans.

Here A. J. P. Taylor is right. The charge of cowardly and short-sighted appeasement leveled at England and France because they gave international sanction to the taking of the *Sudetenland* at Munich in 1938, is itself somewhat unhistorical. Germany had, it is sad to say, arguments which were traditionally acceptable justifications for warlike acts, and honest opinion was much divided. Why should

Chamberlain have gone to war in 1938 to prevent what could be thought of as a dangerous but not irrational adjustment of frontiers? Had not the victorious Allies drawn these borders in defiance of their own principle of national self-determination, and then justified them by hypocritical and dubious theories holding Germany criminally responsible for World War I? Only those who understood the dynamic need for German expansion beyond the *Sudetenland* could have foreseen Hitler's ultimate goal. Our explanations are too simple. Hitler did not take more because no one stopped him from taking less, or because appeasement increases appetite. He took more because he had to have more to reach his implicit social goals.

As for the military logic of the situation, Hitler could have said what Bismarck is reputed to have said on an earlier occasion: "If the British Army lands on the continent, I shall have it arrested." In short, A. J. P. Taylor is again correct when he tells us that the guarantee to Poland, given immediately by Chamberlain when Hitler laid bare his true intentions by seizing non-Sudeten Czechoslovakia, was a rather hasty and somewhat aggressive exercise in futility. The really serious and telling charge that can be leveled against the ruling British and French conservatives was their failure to understand Hitler's need for conquest, and their related unwillingness to join with Bolshevik Russia in making the only kind of military threat that had any chance whatsoever of impeding Hitler. In the event, in late August, 1939, Hitler explained to his generals that Germany must strike without delay. Hitler's reasons were simplicity itself: Only he had the will to carry out the needed conquest and he could not be expected to live forever; Germany's economic position dictated an immediate resolution, and any fear of a blockade should be set aside—the East would provide. Ciano's and Mussolini's last-minute attempts to have war postponed were ignored. The Nonaggression Pact signed by Hitler and Stalin in August, 1939, gave Hitler a free hand to attack France as well as Poland, as long as Stalin was granted his share of the spoils. On September 1, 1939, then, the German and Russian armies invaded Poland.

The defeat of Poland and France was for Hitler no more than a prelude to the attack on the homeland of bolshevism. In spite of many obstacles that might normally have inspired prudence, he moved in 1941. England had not yet been defeated—though, in spite of Churchill's heroic posturing, it was hardly able to intervene in any effective way. Furthermore, German troops had been rushed to the Balkans to protect pro-Fascists in Yugoslavia from a *coup* and to defend Mussolini's troops from an inspired Greek defense. It has been estimated that one-third of the troops sent to Russia could easily have thrown the British out of Egypt. Nevertheless, and ignoring as usual the cautious and, let it be admitted, conservative advice of his generals, Hitler followed what he regarded as his and Germany's destiny. Brushing aside all objections, Hitler instructed his generals to prepare for a new kind of war, a war between ideologies and races, a war which could only be properly fought by those who had discarded obsolete Christian and humanitarian sentiments. Extermination squads were organized and told that tens of millions would have to die. Goering issued the necessary directives. The East was to become a source of supplies for the German war machine. Eventually, 100 million Slavs were to be killed or forced further east to make room for an equal number of Germans, the racial community of the Nordic *Volk.* As his troops poured into Russia on June 22, 1941, Hitler is said to have exclaimed: "Now I feel like a National-Socialist once again." This was Fascist policy pure and uncompromised by traditional conservative reluctance in the face of extremism.

> I shall bring into operation throughout all Europe and the whole world this process of selection which we have carried out through National Socialism in Germany. . . . The vital sections in nations, the militant Nordic sections, will rise again and become the ruling element over these shopkeepers and pacifists, these puritans and speculators. . . . There will not be much left then of the clichés of nationalism, and precious little among even we Germans. Instead there will be an understanding between the various language elements of the one good ruling race.
>
> Hitler, 1934

The most unwelcome truth about the radical right may very well be that they are idealistic and even utopian social visionaries. Hitler felt himself to be the saviour of Nordic humanity, the creator of a new warrior-peasant Europe, a truly new society. He was not unique in this. Before World War I the literature of the radical right contained many such reactionary community models. In 1934, Hitler described his goals. In the middle of Europe there would be a block of 100 million Germans, occupying Germany, Austria, West Poland and Czechoslovakia. Northern France, Belgium, Holland, and Scandinavia would be organized for economic exploitation and complete political subordination. Eastern Poland, the Baltic States, the Ukraine, and the Volga territory would be united in an *Ostbund* of helots—a slave people without independent political, social, economic, or cultural life. Russia would simply cease to exist as a state. The Nordics of Scandinavia and Holland would be used as seedbeds for a vast increase of the race in order to populate the East. All potentially dangerous classes and groups would be destroyed. Extermination squads and induced famine would be employed to alter permanently the "balance of racial forces." The S.S. would become the new nobility of this racial empire, producing Nordic babies while on leave, and using terror to control the subject peoples of

Europe. Europe would become a vast labor reserve of nomadic peoples denied all communal ties and national identity. Under S.S. tutelage Eastern Europe and Russia would become a vast network of governor's palaces and model villages inhabited by the Nordic peasant and warrior aristocracy. What remained of the native population would huddle in the space beyond, in primitive isolation on the edge of starvation.

Correspondingly, in Germany itself Hitler had to go beyond the mere use of totalitarian controls and institutionalized terror in order to preserve the interests of the old "reaction." Furthermore, the Germans were not yet the "master race." Terror, education, and biological selection had first to transform them into a submissive, mindless, and classless mass totally devoid of Christian and humanitarian "weakness." Those who could not be expected to identify with Hitler's new barbarism, whether because of education, religion, race, class, or conviction, were to be destroyed—hence the fate of Socialists, liberals, Communists, intellectuals (when not useful), convinced Christians, reluctant conservatives, Slavs, and even gypsies as well as Jews. For that matter, as I have said, the Nordics themselves were to be purged of all unhealthy strains. As is well known, Hitler had begun the systematic murder of the mentally ill before the war, and it was said that heart, lung, and TB cases were next.

It has often been suggested that fascism has no ideology. In the days of their rise to power, Fascist ideologists tolerated, in aid to that rise, more traditional conservative ideas than they did later. But Nazi ideology at its purest is seen in this crude and violent Social-Darwinist nightmare. Here is to be found the final goal of fascism. It is embodied in the essentially S.S. concept of an heroic, nihilistic warrior elite, coldly exploiting whole populations, populations reduced to an animal-like existence by men themselves purged of their humanity. The concentration camp and the mass grave were not merely examples of Fascist brutality or irrationality, or even simply punitive measures taken against potential enemies of the regime. The concentration camp and the mass grave were to be major governing institutions for implementing the social policies of the thousand-year *Reich.*

Even during the war, Hitler began to implement his grand design. He attempted to recruit, for example, a biological elite from Scandinavia and Holland. Negotiations were begun for the resettlement of five million Dutch farmers in the conquered territories of the East. Subsidies were given to Norwegian women who bore the babies of German soldiers. The S.S. recruited fairly heavily in Holland and Belgium. Léon Degrelle, the leader of Belgium fascism (often mistakenly regarded as a "left" Fascist) called for his followers to cooperate with the S.S. in its attempt to create a "Germanic community." Dutch Fascist units fought on the Eastern front with the Germans. Even in the most favored occupied territories of Scandinavia, however, the extensive and thorough liberal attitudes of the population prevented Nazi attitudes from having anything like general currency. The extreme economic exploitation carried on by the Nazis in all areas, including the West, did not help.

In the East, on the other hand, the Nazis neither expected nor wanted cooperation from the subject peoples. Poland and Russia were to have all vestiges of community life and national consciousness destroyed. Under the notorious Hans Frank, some of the required policies were begun in Poland. Polish intellectuals, landlords, and political leaders were to be slaughtered. Polish literature and even the Polish language were to be obliterated. In Bohemia and Moravia, student leaders were shot, politically minded clergy expelled or killed, and the publication and study of Czech literature and history forbidden. Only unskilled workers and peasant masses were to remain in the East—all higher tasks were reserved for Nordics. Public health measures were to be avoided, food supplies drastically cut, and marriage forbidden among the Slavs. The consequent low birth and high death rates would keep the population at a low level. Communal cultural activities were forbidden, including group dancing and even private parties. At all costs, there was never to be a rise of a new Polish collective consciousness. Such policies were carried to the most terrible extremes by the Germans, yet they were not solely German policies. They were Fascist policies. Rumanian Fascists, for example, carried out murderous genocide policies against the Jews. Bulgarian Fascists attempted to eradicate Greek culture in eastern Macedonia, and strove to resettle at Greek expense thousands of Bulgarians. On a lesser scale, Italians, Austrians, and Lithuanians committed deeds which pale only by comparison with those of the Germans.

In Russia the most terrible extremes of inhumanity became matters of mundane social policy. When detected, Communist officials and party members, as well as Jews, were shot out of hand—often enough by the army. Deliberate starvation policies were carried out. Eventually, the population was to be lowered by tens of millions, and the bulk of the miserable survivors were to be pushed hundreds of miles beyond the Urals. Not even a Nazi Russia could be allowed to exist. As Erich Koch, the prime executor of this program put it, "If I find a Ukranian worthy of sitting at the same table with me, I must have him shot." Even beyond the Urals, the displaced Russians were to be subject to terrible S.S. punitive raids, designed to destroy by terror and force any seeds of a potential community spirit or evidence of its practice. These raids would also, it was hoped, maintain the biological purity of the S.S. itself through selection by battle. Goering, Frank, Koch, and Hitler agreed: 20 or 30 million must die by whatever means during the first two years of German occupation. Hitler ordered Leningrad wiped off the map with Moscow and Stalingrad to follow.

There was never again to be a Russian culture. "They shall do no brain work," Hitler insisted, "or else we shall rear thereby our most determined enemy." Goering advised Koch to have all males over 15 killed in the Ukraine, so as to make room for Nordics. Some military leaders and even Nazis (including the leading ideologist, Alfred Rosenberg) protested that such policies would ruin the excellent chances for organizing Russian anti-Communist units, units in part already in being in the Ukraine. Many army officers may very well have hidden humanitarian sentiments behind such acceptable pragmatic arguments; though the army cooperated freely and it was the famous General von Manstein himself who said that the "Jewish-Bolshevik conspiracy must be crushed forever." The death of some two million Russian prisoners of war hardly indicates oversensitivity to humane considerations. Furthermore, the army played an important role in wiping out whole villages and towns where partisan activity was suspected. Unarmed peasants and women and children were simply shot down on such pacification raids. The military and the S.S. totally destroyed literally thousands of towns, villages, and cities together with their populations. Partisan warfare reached fantastic proportions, but Hitler welcomed this—"It will enable us to destroy vast numbers in reprisals," he remarked. In the end, 30 million may have died in Russia alone. Certainly, it should be remembered that Hitler slaughtered not "merely" 6 million innocent noncombatants, but something more like 20 million.

The sheer horror of these deeds should not cause

us to forget that they were a consequence, if not a necessary consequence, of the economic, political, and social policies the Nazis employed to enforce a social vision generated by the logic of radical right extremism. The crises of the German people could not be explained or remedied except by reference to the complexities of a modern society caught in a dialectic of extremes—and needing structural and liberal reform. But the radical right is brought to power by those to whom such modern social change is a threat, a mortal threat. Hence the need, as we have seen, for congenital enemies—international conspirators who by nature cannot be transformed or reformed, but only destroyed. The logic of Nazi internal policy, in short, led to the policies implied in the words of Koch, Nazi ruler of Russia:

> We are the master race. We must remember that the lowliest German worker is racially and biologically a thousand times more valuable than the population here.

CONCLUDING SPECULATIONS

The search for a narrow and exclusive definition of fascism has been pressed too hard. As a variety of right-wing extremism, fascism must always adapt itself to the unique conservative traditions and values of the particular society it hopes to dominate. Each nation, as it were, generates the fascism it deserves.[1] Hence, it is imperative that fascism be studied on an international scale. The reader will know from what has preceded of my own serious doubts as to the prospects for the radical right in liberalized-consensus societies. Nevertheless, this *may* be basically a question of the magnitude and nature of the social crises involved. Both the well-armed Minutemen and the respectable upper-middle class Birchites are, after all, not exceedingly dissimilar to German radical right and non-Nazi groups which, at crucial moments in the 1930s, merged their votes and members with Hitler's legions. Unlike the Minutemen, the Birchites are not officially anti-Semitic, nor do they ask now for a military dictatorship to ward off what they call the internal threat of Communism. Without doubting the sincerity of their ideological statements, one may

[1] If the American Nazi party is any example, a fascist movement may very well lose whatever potential it may have by mindlessly aping foreign models and thus offending the local radical rightists—in this case, the Birchites, Buckleyites, and Minutemen.

point out that fascism in America is more likely to vent its racist attitudes on Negroes. As it is, the Birch Society argues that the Negro occupies an inferior position in America because he *is* inferior, genetically inferior. As for the Civil Rights Movement, the Birchites regard it as simply and in every branch a part of the internal Communist conspiracy. How massive and successful would the Civil Rights Movement have to become in Alabama, say, before the genteel conservatives and "moderate" racists decide that more than the casual terrorism of the southern judiciary and police will be necessary? The reader will recall that I titled this section, "concluding speculations." I have not forgotten that Alabama is attached to the United States and that already the defenders of southern womanhood find it hard to sustain their version of fascist ideology, *viz.*, that the civil rights liberalism which threatens them is really the result of an external invasion of Communists and racial degenerates who are corrupting their happy lower classes with alien values. Still, it is legitimate to speculate about the potential explosive power of a radical-right reaction in the United States which, without adopting the trappings of European models, has grown strong by feeding on the status anxieties of *nouveaux riches* and lower-middle class elements; the progress of civil rights and social welfare legislation; and above all the American government's self-defined defeats at the hands, it is supposed, of a centrally directed international Communist conspiracy which has already seized the teeming millions of China from our grasp.

My own judgment and knowledge, however, lead me to suspect that the greatest potential for fascism lies not in the liberal West, but rather in the dialectical polarities even now increasing in non-Western or underdeveloped societies. I hasten to repeat again that this section is meant to be tentative and speculative. We should recall, nevertheless, that in late nineteenth-century Russia, for example, there were violent, reactionary, and murderously anti-Semitic movements, as with the famous *Black Hundreds*. If the "Whites" had defeated the Bolsheviks in the Civil War, would a simple return to traditional Tzarist authoritarianism have been enough to contain the radical discontent of the peasant masses, or would the revolutionary and totalitarian potential of the radical right have been needed? Ignorance prevents me from offering even a tentative answer. Fascistic movements are to be found in many non-Western societies. If they are to be understood and kept from power, comparative knowledge and judgments become essential. Nor are we completely lacking now in the evidence and analogy relevant to assessing the fascist potential of non-Western societies. Europe is not the only society in which liberalism and radicalism have confronted powerful remnants of feudalism and upper class reaction in the rapid drive toward modernization and industrialism. May not the Japanese example prove instructive if not decisive?

The crucial question is not, as is often assumed, whether or not Japan in the 1930s was ruled by fascists or simply by traditional Japanese reactionary militarism, a question on which there is no unanimity among Japanese scholars. Japan did have powerful and popular fascist movements which were close to the European model, and responsive to roughly similar pressures. Japanese history had seen its feudal era, its absolute and bureaucratic state, and, later, its powerful but obsolete and privileged warrior class—armed retainers of the landed aristocracy. Not unlike their occurrence in Germany, industrialism and modernism came to Japan with startling swiftness. Their advent provoked not only tentative moves toward liberalism, but also a powerful right-wing, ultranationalist, and militaristic counterreaction, led by the aristocracy. The leading groups in Japan, having abolished feudalism and introduced Bismarck-like constitutional arrangements, did not want liberalism from the West. They *did* want science, technology, and above all, weapons in order to keep Japan for the Japanese and their complex and unique traditional cultural values. Similarly, after World War I, Japan was apparently in the firm control of civilian, liberal, and Western-oriented politicians. The introduction of manhood suffrage (in 1925) completed an increasing liberal danger to the old ways and classes. Furthermore, Japan was a revisionist power after the settlements of the war and, for that matter, had far better reasons to resent Allied oppression than Germany or Italy; for Japan's unequal treaties dated back to the 1850s. All of this had predictable consequences. In the interwar period, a counterreaction—militaristic, imperialistic, ultranationalist, and violently antiliberal—was spearheaded by the aristocracy, the army, and independent fascist groups usually composed of petty-bourgeois ultrapatriotic associations and the especially violent and determined associations of junior army officers. Financial and moral support seems to have come from many of those business interests which stood to play an important role in the exploitation of imperial territories, and from lower-middle class and medium-owning peasant groups.

The "founder of Japanese fascism" was Kita Ikki. His *Plan for the Reorganization of Japan* contains many of the fascist ideas we have already discussed. He called for a military dictatorship, an end to class warfare, total internal unity, the destruction of "un-Japanese" Western liberalism and socialism, and above all the creation by armed force of a vast "New Order" to include both China and India. Such extreme imperialism, however, was not new to Japanese military and political leaders. Japan's swiftly expanding population and her complete dependence on exports and imports had led to a fairly general belief that only through the establishment of a "coprosperity sphere" at the expense of the British and Russian empires could Japan resolve her domestic crises. By 1931, in any event, Japan pushed into Manchuria. In 1937, a full scale invasion of China was underway. Meanwhile, liberal and radical groups were disciplined and punished by a government increasingly dominated by the military. Yet, this was by no means an out-and-out fascist take-over, and the radical right was never satisfied with such traditionalists as Tojo. Nevertheless, it is not difficult to understand why, during the heat of battle, Western observers made no such careful distinctions.

If fascism is to become a tradition, then it will find its most likely social base, I believe, in such dialectical confrontations of new left and old right in underdeveloped countries. Comparative studies on a truly international scale are absolutely necessary. What *are* we to make of the contemporary fascistic movements in Latin America? What will be the response of the ruling, racist, and white minority in Rhodesia if social development and political awareness among the black masses lead to a fearful confrontation? Is it true, as Brian Bunting tells us in his *The Rise of the South African Reich*, that the late Verwoerd and the white government's Nationalist party had increasingly and deliberately adopted the practice and spirit of the Nazis? Is this the ultimate meaning of South African racial laws, police terror, arbitrary detention, trade union controls, the elimination of opposition, and mass indoctrination? Will fascism have its Lenin, that is, one who adopts a European ideology to the social conditions of underdeveloped and peasant lands? Was this, for example, what occurred under Codreanu's leadership in Rumania? I think we assume too readily that social conditions in non-Western nations automatically favor left totalitarianism.

Hitler hoped to pull the West down with him to defeat. He may yet succeed. One of the consequences of the Nazi rise to power was the invention of atomic weaponry and missile systems. The social policy of fascism, as I have said, is one of international war. We may use our ultimate weapons systems without the stimulus of fascist success in other lands. It is true that escalation in limited wars between nuclear powers may very well lead to a rational backdown on the part of one or the other of the hostile parties. As an historian I find this hard to believe. At least all will admit that there are other possibilities. What are the odds on these "other possibilities" if a new Mussolini or Hitler should gain power? For this compelling reason alone we must use our knowledge and scholarship to investigate the fascist potential in non-Western lands. Europe is unique, but the European experience is becoming common. In non-Western lands feudal traditionalists and conservative upper-middle classes increasingly must face the full implications of what we now call the "revolution of rising expectations"—a revolution occurring among masses previously fairly easy to manage. How many of these threatened ruling groups will seek a fascist way out? And what are we to say of Western nations, such as the United States, which deny their own liberal tradition by supporting reactionary feudalism in underdeveloped nations? Do they not contribute directly to the rise of the radical right? History is a useful science. The past *can* tell us something of the future. The historian's wisdom may be the wisdom of hindsight. But if we look back we can study the rise of European fascism. Such is the variety of history, that our hindsight may very easily become as well a glimpse into the future. Let us hope instead that it becomes a means for shaping our fate.

SELECTED BIBLIOGRAPHY OF PAPERBOUND EDITIONS

THE COMPARATIVE STUDY OF INTERNATIONAL FASCISM

Such studies are unfortunately rare. Only now are scholars beginning to shake off their obsession with the nation-state as the basic historical unit. The following books are all, however, very helpful.

ARENDT, HANNAH. *The Origins of Totalitarianism* (Meridan Books, 1958). A famous and fascinating book which has had a mighty influence on all those concerned with fascism. In my opinion, however, Hannah Arendt overemphasizes the irrational nature of Naziism, and relates it too directly to the dilemma of "modern man" in industrial society, rather than specific men in specific social situations. Thus, Miss Arendt makes much of the isolation and alienation of men who, presumably, have lost their class identity and, in a search for psychological security, may easily identify with political movements which make monolithic claims. In my opinion, the rise of the Nazis was much more a result of class identity, class fears, and the struggle of class interests.

Correspondingly, Miss Arendt overrates the importance of anti-Semitism in fascist movements. She does not see that for the radical right, ultraconservatism is primary and anti-Semitism secondary. And in spite of the terrible deeds committed, fascist anti-Semitism was rational in the sense that it was a result of the conservative struggle to end the threat of liberalism and radicalism; a threat closely associated in Central and Eastern Europe with the overrepresentation of Jews in the modern sectors of society. Miss Arendt's sense of the essential irrationality of fascism, leads her to emphasize totalitarian institutions and the techniques of social control and to neglect the class basis of social policies. She ignores basic differences between left and right totalitarianism, and even argues that Fascist Italy was not really totalitarian—all this because she believes fascism is not a product of the politics of class and status, and must ape the German model.

Having said all this, however, I hasten to add that this large book contains a wide range of unequaled and breathtaking insights into the social psychology of totalitarian rule and the political manipulation of personality. Hence *The Origins of Totalitarianism,* in spite of my complaints, is basic to the study of the radical right in power. Like all of Miss Arendt's books, it is a must.

LIPSET, SEYMOUR MARTIN. *Political Man: The Social Bases of Politics* (Anchor, 1963). Although there is only one section on fascism in Mr. Lipset's book, it ought to be included in this listing. For Mr. Lipset has summarized the results of much extremely important work done by others on the voting behavior of Germans during the rise to power of the Nazis. Unfortunately, Mr. Lipset's lack of knowledge of German political and party life has misled him into thinking that the liberal middle classes rather than traditional conservatives played the major role in the success of the Nazis. As we have seen, however, traditional conservatives did not need to switch their votes to Hitler (though many did) because increasingly their own party programs resembled his. Moreover, it is incorrect to regard as truly liberal the small German middle class parties which saw their voters desert to the Nazis in the early 1930s. Their programs did not extend beyond the absolute defense of private property against all liberal social welfare measures. They might more properly be regarded as akin to our own Birchite conservatives and radical right in general.

MOSSE, GEORGE L. and WALTER LAQUEUR, Editors. *The Journal of Contemporary History, International Fascism, 1920–1945* (Volume 1, No. 1, 1966). This is the first issue of what will certainly become the outstanding journal in its field. (It has been issued as a paperback.) It contains ten articles by different scholars on various aspects of fascism in France, Italy, Spain, Austria, Rumania, and elsewhere; and also general articles by men of the caliber of George L. Mosse and Hugh

Seton-Watson. Altogether a worthy enterprise. Students of contemporary history will appreciate the editors' interest in broad general topics, and their refusal to follow the sterile drift toward narrow specialization.

WEBER, EUGENE. *Varieties of Fascism* (Anvil Original, 1964). A review of fascism and national socialism in Italy, Germany, Rumania, Hungary, Spain, Belgium, France, and Great Britain. Basic information is combined with selected documents from the programs and speeches of leading European right-wing extremists. Mr. Weber does not share my belief that fascism can be unambiguously classified as a rightist conservative movement. In turn, I believe that Mr. Weber is too willing to accept the ideological statements of Fascists at face value, and hence takes their "leftism" far more seriously than he should. In power, and when coming close to power, fascists jettisoned their own left elements and retained only those lower-middle-class anticapitalist ideas which, in reality, were a variety of European conservative thought. Furthermore, Mr. Weber tends to overrate the significance of marginal worker support of fascism, and also seems to confuse distinctions between industrial workers and craft and guildsmen. Nevertheless, Mr. Weber ought to be read, both because of his brilliance for its own sake, and because he is the best representative of the opposition to many of the views I have expressed in the text.

GERMANY, THE WEIMAR REPUBLIC, AND THE RISE OF THE NAZIS

BULLOCK, ALAN. *Hitler: A Study in Tyranny* (Bantam Books, rev. ed., 1961). This it without doubt the single best work available not only on Hitler, but on the political and social history of his rise to power, his rule, and his destruction. By general agreement, this book is a masterful product of the historical imagination at its best. The reader ought to avoid the current shorter versions of this work, and avail himself of the complete and revised edition. It has no equal.

DELARUE, JACQUES. *The Gestapo* (Dell, 1965). The history of the secret state police of the Nazis, with a thorough, detailed, and horrifying discussion of its leadership, its internal terrorist functions, and its occupation policies.

HALPERIN, S. WILLIAM. *Germany Tried Democracy* (Norton, 1965). There is no better book for the reader who wants both a thorough narrative of the political history of the Weimar Republic and an intelligent analysis of that history. The book is large in size, evidence, narrative, and spirit.

HITLER, ADOLF. *Mein Kampf* (Riverside Press, two Volumes in one, 1943 [originally published in 1925]). For those who want to go directly to the source, and those who still dismiss Hitler as psychotic.

JARMAN, T. L. *The Rise and Fall of Nazi Germany* (Cresset Press, 1955). A useful narrative of the rise of the Nazis to power in Germany, with the usual, but somewhat superficial, explanations: Hitler's demonic will, German nationalism, the Great Depression and the "failure" of the West to carry out vigorous anti-Nazi policies.

LEWY, GUENTER. *The Catholic Church and Nazi Germany* (McGraw-Hill, 1965). The best work in this much-argued topic. With scholarly care, Mr. Lewy shows that there was much sympathy with National Socialism among the Church leadership. Such sympathy was generated by the Church's general support of traditional conservative and organic-state theories (see Father Coughlin's *Social Justice* and Leo XIII's *Rerum Novarum*) and its general opposition to liberal modernism. The Church was, after all, part of the German conservative establishment, and therefore shared its nationalistic, autocratic, and antileftist attitudes. With some important exceptions, the Catholic Church supported conservative movements as a balance to liberal, socialist, and agnostic Weimar. The only mystery about all this is why liberals should expect the Church to do otherwise.

LOCKNER, LOUIS P. (trans. and ed.). *The Goebbels Diaries* (Eagle Books, 1948). A fascinating and extensive collection of Propaganda Minister Goebbels' personal writings from 1942 through 1943—the crucial years for Nazi leadership. This was the time of the turning point of the war from apparent German victory to threatening defeat. The book reveals much of Goebbels personality, and the petty jealousies and rivalries of the Nazi leadership.

MAYER, MILTON. *They Thought They Were Free: The Germans, 1933–1945* (Phoenix Press, Chicago, 1965). An absorbing study of a small number of Germans who became Nazis, written by one who knew them well. The author's ability to understand the social frustrations and values of those who drifted into the Nazi camp makes the book invaluable. Mr. Mayer's refusal to take the easy moralizing way out is especially helpful. As E. H. Carr has said, the problem in history is not to understand why bad men do evil, but why good men do evil.

MEINECKE, FRIEDRICH. *The German Catastrophe* (Beacon, 1963). These reflections and recollections of Germany's most honored historian (and an anti-Nazi) show only too well how difficult it is for a participant to understand the history of his own generation. Ignoring fundamental differences between the left and the right, and the lower-middle class masses as versus the proletariat, Meinecke blames the rise of Hitler on mass democracy when, in reality, it seems more the product of the lack of it. Meinecke argues that the German public was conditioned to authoritarianism by the collectivist notions of the German Socialist party, and that this is one of the main sources of German authoritarian attitudes inherited by Hitler. To say this, however, is to ignore the autocratic collectivism of the far older and more powerful German conservative tradition, and the essentially reformist and pragmatic spirit of the German Socialists.

Furthermore, it is simply incorrect to argue, as does Meinecke, that the socialism of *National Socialism* was a leftist phenomenon. Meinecke's own respectable and genteel conservatism perhaps betrayed him here.

MOSSE, GEORGE L. *The Crisis of German Ideology: Intellectual Origins of the Third Reich* (Universal Library, 1964). This book is an absolute must for those who want to know the history and scope of right-wing radical nationalism and anti-Semitism in modern Germany, and before Hitler. All classes, groups, associations, institutions and elites are investigated with rare skill by Mr. Mosse. The results, if depressing, shatter forever any notion of Hitler's originality or uniqueness in the Germanic life of the spirit. The book itself is a valuable example of how intellectual history ought to be written by those who want to understand social movements.

NEUMANN, FRANZ. *Behemoth: The Structure and Practice of National Socialism* (Forthcoming in a paperback edition). A famous work which deserves to be so. Neumann argued that the Nazi seizure of power was essentially a counterrevolution of imperialistic monopoly capitalists and reactionary big landowners against democracy and social progress. The central drive behind the Nazis was for Neumann the ever more urgent drive for imperialistic conquest as a function of the growth of monopolization. In my opinion, however, German capitalists were imperialistic not because it is the nature of monopoly capitalism to be so, but because capitalism in Germany grew in an environment dominated by preliberal elites and values which stressed the importance and dignity of war and conquest. Furthermore, I believe Neumann underestimated the role of other groups which aided the Nazis to power: army officers, civil servants, small businessmen, etc. Certainly, Neumann was well aware of their influence; it is a matter of emphasis. Neumann sacrificed his awareness of the pluralistic sources of Nazi support because of his single-minded absorption with advanced capitalism as the driving force behind fascism.

As a Social Democrat, trade union lawyer, and political activist during Weimar, Neumann also tended to overrate the tactical and strategic errors of the liberal and left opposition to the radical right. Given the position and power of old and new conservatives in Germany it seems hardly possible that the Social Democrats, even had they led a united and politically wise left, could ever have presented an unsurmountable obstacle to the right. Neumann's critique of their role depends too much on his underemphasis on the pluralistic sources of support for the radical right and on his preoccupation with monopoly capitalism.

The Social Democrats in any case have been blamed too much for their "failure" to stop fascism. Such accusations rest on a misreading of the latent power of the right in times of social crisis in Western nations, and a mistaken view of the potentials of the left. It ought to be said, however, that Neumann's critique of the left is far more valid than that, say, of a Trotsky—who once put it thus:

> We may set it down as an historical law: Fascism was able to conquer only in those countries where the conservative labor parties prevented the proletariat from utilizing the revolutionary situation and seizing power.

SHIRER, WILLIAM L. *The Rise and Fall of the Third Reich* (Crest, 1963). The most well-known popular narrative history of the Nazis. Its vast size, however, does not seem necessary, even though much interesting information is to be found therein. Mr. Shirer tends to sacrifice causal analysis for popular narrative. Still, he must be given full credit for having created a vast public interest in the *Third Reich*. In general, however, Mr. Shirer relies too much on the clichés of the 1940s—clichés which tend to overstate specific German responsibility for fascism, and ignore its general European aspects.

SNELL, JOHN L. (ed.). *The Nazi Revolution: Germany's Guilt or Germany's Fate* (D. C. Heath, 1959). Selections from 18 scholars, all of whom represent varying views as to the reasons for the success of the Nazis. Interesting and useful, especially to those weaned on textbook absolutism. Like all such books, of course, it suffers from a lack of the complete arguments and evidence presented by the authors excerpted.

TAYLOR, A. J. P. *The Course of German History* (Putnam, 1962). Perhaps the best, certainly the most controversial, general discussion of modern German history, from 1815 through Hitler. Mr. Taylor shows with his usual brilliance that the ideological attitudes and political practices which brought about the *Third Reich* had deep roots in the German past, and especially among the traditional ruling elites caught in the social turmoil of the 1920s and 1930s. Mr. Taylor at his best, and his best is unbeatable.

ITALY, MUSSOLINI, AND THE FASCISTS

FERMI, LAURA. *Mussolini* (Phoenix Paperbacks, 1964). Thorough, judicious, and intelligent.

FINER, HERMAN. *Mussolini's Italy* (Universal Library,. 1965). Although originally published in 1935 and not revised, Mr. Finer's book is still a reliable guide to the social policies and totalitarian institutions of Fascist Italy. Mr. Finer shows how the administrative, educational, institutional, and economic arrangements under Mussolini were designed so as to uphold the rule of the landed and business elites in the face of the postwar advance of liberalism and radicalism in Italy.

HALPERIN, S. WILLIAM. *Mussolini and Italian Fascism* (Anvil Original, 1964). An excellent basic introduction to Italian Fascism—an informed, judicious, and intelligent narrative with a good selection of source readings. The kind of work historians ought to undertake more often for the benefit of the intelligent and interested layman.

FASCISM IN SPAIN AND EASTERN EUROPE

PAYNE, STANLEY G. *Falange: A History of Spanish Fascism* (Stanford University Press, 1961). A descriptive study of the *Falange* in Spain, with most attention given to the political maneuvers and countermaneuvers of the interwar period. Unfortunately, the book is weak on social analysis and contains only scattered and uncertain information as to the appeal of Spanish Fascism to the different classes of Spain. Similarly, the reader who is unacquainted with Spain's unique social structure will find it difficult to understand the meaning of the political narrative, as he may very well misinterpret terms familiar to him only through knowledge of liberal Western nations.

SETON-WATSON, HUGH. *The East European Revolution* (Praeger, 1951). Packed full of intelligently presented materials relevant to the social structure and politics of Eastern Europe, this book is indispensable for those who want to understand the prevalence of radical right ideas and practices in Poland, Rumania, and Hungary. It is especially valuable in its coverage of the social role of the peasantry, landed aristocracy, and new bourgeois, as well as the social bases of ultranationalism and anti-Semitism in Eastern Europe.

THOMAS, HUGH. *The Spanish Civil War* (Harper Colophon Book, 1965). A solid narrative, but overwritten and a little too unthematic for clarity. The reader must do some of the author's work in order to organize the material. Mr. Thomas has attempted to maintain a strict neutrality about this controversial tragedy, but has been, I think, unfair to the Republic. (Although not as yet in paperback, Gabriel Jackson's *The Spanish Republic and the Civil War* [Princeton University Press, 1966] is highly recommended as a counterbalance.)

WAR AND THE FOREIGN POLICY OF FASCISM

LOEWENHEIM, FRANCIS L. (ed.). *Peace or Appeasement? Hitler, Chamberlain, and Munich* (Houghton, Mifflin, 1965). A selection of views relative to the attempted settlement of the Sudetenland question at Czechoslovakian expense at the famous Munich Conference of 1938. In my opinion, the importance of Munich is much overrated, as I tried to show in the text. We could do with a selection of views as to why the Allies could not, or would not, cooperate with Russia, or vice versa, for an effective check to Hitler. Failing that alliance, the allied surrender at Munich was inevitable.

TAYLOR, A. J. P. *Origins of the Second World War* (Fawcett, 1963). This unfortunate book shows the impossibility of treating Hitler's foreign policy as a traditional policy of interest of states, divorced from any consideration of internal pressures and the social dynamics which made war and imperialism a necessity. Paradoxically, as I have noted earlier, this book contradicts what Mr. Taylor himself had already said some years before in *The Course of German History*. Nevertheless, Mr. Taylor does throw much new light on the various clichés by which liberal historians have argued that Western appeasement decisively encouraged Nazi aggression. In short, even working with a wrong-headed theme Mr. Taylor is able to increase our understanding of diplomatic history. The reader will learn much of value if he pays more attention to what Mr. Taylor says, rather than his somewhat flip way of saying it.

WERTH, ALEXANDER. *Russia at War, 1941–45* (Avon Books, 1964). A magnificent, monumental, and intensely interesting 1000-page study of Russia at war—a study which goes far beyond mere military history and relates the social impact of the war on Russia. Written with the unique skill, thoroughness, and intelligence we have come to associate with the work of Alexander Werth.

FASCISM AND ANTI-SEMITISM

PULZER, PETER G. J. *The Rise of Political Anti-Semitism in Germany and Austria* (Wiley, 1964). An excellent analysis of the political expressions of anti-Semitism in Central Europe, especially thorough for the period from 1870 to World War II. With great skill Mr. Pulzer shows how conservative and lower-middle class liberalism, antiliberalism, and ultranationalism became focused on anti-Semitism, and permeated all sorts of social groups, clubs, leagues, and informal associations. The book contains valuable information about the political alliances formed between traditional conservatives and radical rightists during times of social crisis.

REITLINGER, GERALD. *The Final Solution: The Attempt to Exterminate the Jews of Europe, 1939–45* (A. S. Barnes, 1961). A thorough study of the techniques used by the Nazis to murder the Jews of Europe, with a discussion of the fate of the Jews in each area of Europe under German occupation. This study throws much light on the dark means of political and social control and the dehumanization policies under totalitarian rule.

THE PSYCHOLOGICAL APPEAL OF FASCISM AND TOTALITARIANISM

ADORNO, T. W., and others. *The Authoritarian Personality,* Parts One and Two (Science Edition Paperbacks, John Wiley, 1964). A lengthy and famous study of the psychology of the authoritarian personality, based on extensive data collected from tests, interviews, and case studies. The book explores in depth the kind of personality most likely to be attracted to totalitarian political movements, and explores the relationship between psychological traits and antidemocratic, ultranationalistic, and anti-Semitic attitudes. The book is unfortunately marred by much vague jargonizing, but valuable if read selectively. (See especially the fascinating case histories, the section on fascism, and the Conclusion.)

BARBU, ZEVEDIE. *Democracy and Dictatorship: Their Psychology and Pattern of Life* (Evergreen Books, 1956). Fascism is here regarded as of overwhelming appeal to those suffering the stresses and strains of the interwar years in Europe, especially when circumstances are such as to deprive people of their institutional, social, or class identity and security. Thus the unemployed worker, the defeated war veteran, the alienated student, the desperate lower-middle class businessman, and the aristocrat bereft of his power, Barbu argues, all surrendered to Naziism by force of the attraction of opposites. The Nazis offered security to those who had none, pride to the humbled, heroism to the fearful, and world mastery to the victims of social chaos.

FROMM, ERICH. *Escape From Freedom* (Avon, 1965). This is a general discussion of the psychological appeal of totalitarianism in our time. It includes remarks about the appeal of the Nazis to the German people. Those who resisted the Nazis but weakly, Mr. Fromm contends, were neutralized because they suffered from an "inner tiredness and resignation" which affects modern man in general. As for those who were active Nazi supporters, mainly the lower-middle class, Mr. Fromm regards them as attracted to the Nazis by their love of the strong and hatred of the weak; their pettiness and hostility; their narrow patriotism; and their inability to express their emotions in a tolerant, broad, and humane way. Much of this admittedly valuable psychologizing seems to me to result not so much from scientific insight on Mr. Fromm's part, but from his lack of sympathy with the character of the German lower-middle class, and is hardly the final word.

INDEX

71 72 73 12 11 10 9 8 7